The IBM PC Made Easy

Prentice-Hall Personal Computing Series
Lance A. Leventhal, series editor

Fabbri, *Animation, Games, and Graphics For The Timex-1000*
Fabbri, *Animation, Games, and Sound For The Apple II/IIe*
Fabbri, *Animation, Games, and Sound For The IBM PC*
Fabbri, *Animation, Games, and Sound For The VIC-20*
Harris & Scofield, *IBM PC Conversion Handbook of Basic*
Scanlon, *The IBM PC Made Easy*
Schnapp & Stafford, *Computer Graphics For The Timex 1000 and Sinclair ZX-81*

THE IBM PC MADE EASY

Leo J. Scanlon

Prentice-Hall, Inc.
Englewood Cliffs, NJ 07632

Library of Congress Cataloging in Publication Data

Scanlon, Leo J.
The IBM PC made easy.

(Prentice-Hall personal computing series)
Includes index.
1. IBM Personal Computer—Programming. 2. Basic (Computer program language) I. Title. II. Series.
QA76.8.I2594S33 1984 001.64′2 83-21314
ISBN 0-13-448473-8
ISBN 0-13-448465-7 (pbk.)

Editorial/production supervision and
interior design: Kathryn Gollin Marshak
Cover design: Photo Plus Art—Celine Brandes
Manufacturing buyer: Gordon Osbourne
Photo credit: John Wait

Printed in the United States of America

10 9 8 7 6 5 4 3 2 1

ISBN 0-13-448465-7 {PBK.}
ISBN 0-13-448473-8 {CASE}

Prentice-Hall International, Inc., *London*
Prentice-Hall of Australia Pty. Limited, *Sydney*
Editora Prentice-Hall do Brasil, Ltda., *Rio de Janeiro*
Prentice-Hall Canada Inc., *Toronto*
Prentice-Hall of India Private Limited, *New Delhi*
Prentice-Hall of Japan, Inc., *Tokyo*
Prentice-Hall of Southeast Asia Pte. Ltd., *Singapore*
Whitehall Books Limited, *Wellington, New Zealand*

CONTENTS

PREFACE

This book is a practical guide to the IBM Personal Computer (PC). By "practical," we mean that the book discusses things PC owners need to know. We do not try to cover every last detail of the computer (the manuals you get with the PC do *that*), just the essential points. We also describe some options you might want to add to your PC.

Along the way, we introduce the fundamentals of programming, in case you want to write some simple programs on your own. Although you will generally use purchased programs for major jobs, you might occasionally write short programs for minor jobs like calculating a golf handicap, converting liters to quarts, or producing fancy meeting notices. There are also specialized jobs for which you are unlikely to find programs you can buy. Typical examples include preparing logs for pilots or navigators, comparing alternative government aid formulas, and determining the amount of pipe or wire a building will need.

In short, this book tells you what you need to know to use the PC to its full advantage. After all, you spent a lot of money for this machine; you might as well get all you paid for.

THE INTENDED AUDIENCE

This book assumes you have never used a computer. With this in mind, we explain everything in ordinary English and use technical terms only when absolutely necessary. Furthermore, we progress at a relaxed pace and introduce new topics only when you need to know about them.

Again, we do not try to force irrelevant or complex material on you. Instead, we just present the essentials of a given topic and tell you where to find advanced explanations if you want to go further.

WHAT THIS BOOK CONTAINS

This book has five chapters. In Chapter 1, Computer Components, we take a brief survey of the equipment and programs you get with the computer and suggest options you may want to buy later. Chapter 2, Getting Started, tells you what to do when you turn on the PC. It also describes *disks*, which hold the programs the PC runs.

Chapter 3, BASIC, introduces you to the BASIC programming language. Here you can learn how to write simple programs. Besides being a sophisticated accounting machine, word processor, and so on, the PC is also a superb calculator.

Chapter 4, Disk Operating System, helps you to use disks efficiently. Chapter 5, Sound, Graphics, and Color, is a special extension of Chapter 3. It shows you how to write programs that produce sounds, and even tunes, through the PC's built-in speaker. It also shows you how to write programs that draw pictures on the screen.

There are three appendices to the book that summarize material within the book and help you to look up details quickly.

Finally, on a personal note, I would like to thank Dr. Lance Leventhal and Ms. Paula Criswell of PC Editorial Services for making substantial improvements to my manuscript. I must also thank Mr. John Wait of Prentice-Hall and Mr. Dow Postle of ComputerLand in Ocala, Florida, for their enthusiastic support.

Happy computing!

Leo J. Scanlon

The IBM PC Made Easy

Chapter 1

COMPUTER COMPONENTS

Your IBM Personal Computer (also called PC) is made up of two things: *hardware* (the physical equipment) and *software* (the programs that tell the computer what to do). Before we discuss the details of the PC, let's examine its hardware and software components.

1.1 HARDWARE

Every PC has at least four hardware items: the computer itself (IBM calls it the "System Unit"), the keyboard, a video display or television set, and either a cassette tape recorder or a disk drive. The cassette recorder and the disk drive do the same thing, but the disk drive is much more convenient to use. Optional hardware items include a printer, game controllers (paddles or joysticks), a modem (for communicating by telephone), and a light pen (for indicating points on the display screen).

Computer

The computer itself is a rectangular gray and white typewriter-sized object. It has a flat top, air vents in front and back, and a recess that holds the disk drives. Its only distinguishing characteristic, other than its IBM label, is a red power switch on the right-hand side near the back. This switch is out of the way because you won't want to turn the computer on or off very often.

As a computer user, you need not be concerned about the computer's insides any more than you need to be concerned about the insides of a washing machine, refrigerator, or television set. Simply for your education (or curiosity), we should say that the computer has

1. A brain, usually called a *central processing unit* (*CPU*). You sometimes see this referred to as a *microprocessor* or, in the case of the PC, as an 8088 microprocessor. The 8088 is simply a model number.
2. Some memory, for remembering facts (data) and procedures (programs). Computer memory comes in units called *bytes*; each byte can hold one typed character. PCs typically have many thousands of bytes of memory, so we refer to the total memory in terms of *Ks* (1K = 1024 bytes, but you can just think of it as 1000).

   PCs usually come with 48K or 64K of memory, but some may have as much as 512K. Ask your dealer if you are not sure how much memory your PC has.
3. Connections for the attached devices, such as the video display, keyboard, and cassette recorder. These connections act like the body's muscles and nerves. We call them *interfaces*, and we call the attached devices *peripherals*.

Such terms as CPU, microprocessor, byte, K, interface, and peripheral are common computer jargon. You might as well get used to them, since you will see them in manuals, books, and magazines. We will try to explain each term as we need it. Besides, these are good terms to use in polite conversation to let people know that you are now a computer expert.

Keyboard

Unlike the Apple II or Radio Shack TRS-80, the PC does not have a built-in keyboard. Instead, the keyboard is separate and connects to the computer through a coiled cable. This separation lets you hold the keyboard in your lap or move it around. You can also unplug the keyboard to prevent children and other curiosity seekers from using it without your knowledge.

The keys are arranged in three groups, as shown in Figure 1-1. The white keys in the center are like those on a typewriter. The lowercase letters are present, even though they do not appear on the keys. There are a few extra symbols, too, such as ¦, \, [, and].

The dark keys immediately next to the white letter and symbol keys are control keys. Some of these are also familiar to a typist, although the markings are different. The keys marked with upward-pointing arrows are shifts, which you use to type capital letters or uppercase symbols. The key with a bent left arrow is Return or Enter; here it not only concludes the current line but also enters it into the computer. The left arrow key is a backspace, which is used most often to delete characters from the display as it moves left.

The other dark keys are not on a typewriter. Most of them are used to enter programs or to do things that make sense on a video display but not on a typewriter, such as erasing an entire line. Caps Lock is a handy variation on a shift lock key; it locks in capital letters *but leaves the non-letter keys in lowercase.*

Be careful with Caps Lock. Pressing it once locks in capital letters, but pressing it again returns the keyboard to lowercase. There is no way of telling which case is active except by pressing a key. Furthermore, if you press a shift key and a letter key when Caps Lock is active, the letter key will be lowercase! Nonletter keys always work normally.

The white keys at the right are like the keys on a calculator. We call them a *numeric keypad*, because they are commonly used to enter long sequences of numbers (such as item prices, grades, or population figures). The regular number keys in the typewriter section are also available, but their positions would make heavy use awkward.

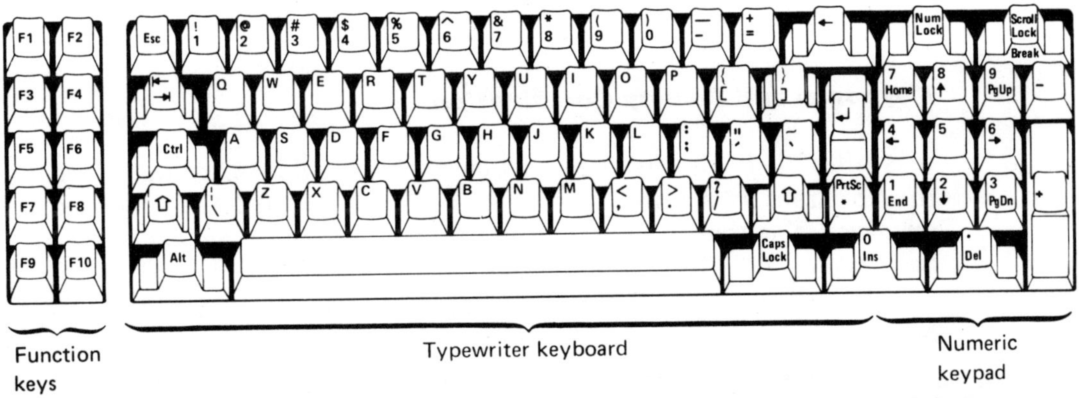

Figure 1-1. The IBM Personal Computer keyboard (Courtesy of IBM Corporation)

Note that the keys in the numeric keypad also have uppercase markings. Pressing the Num Lock key changes these keys from one case to the other. As with Caps Lock, you can only tell which case is active by pressing a key.

The dark keys at the far left are *function keys*, labeled F1 through F10. These serve as shorthand ways to tell the computer to perform entire procedures. The function keys can save you a lot of typing (as you will see later), but they are more an occasional convenience than a necessity.

Display

There are several different kinds of video displays (like television sets) that may be attached to your PC. You may have an IBM Monochrome Display (like a black-and-white television, except that it shows green characters on a black background), an IBM Color/Graphics Monitor, or a standard television set or television monitor.

As far as ordinary typing is concerned, all video displays are the same; they show 25 lines of 80 characters. You can think of this as a grid consisting of 25 lines or rows and 80 columns. In reality, only 24 lines are available to you, since the computer uses the bottom line for its own special purposes.

If you want to draw pictures or figures (*graphics*) with your computer, the various displays have different characteristics. The Color/Graphics Monitor or television set lets you control tiny dots (320 or 640 horizontally, 200 vertically) to create highly detailed pictures. The Monochrome Display lets you put only simple, letter-sized shapes in the normal 25-by-80-character grid.

Keyboard and Display Combination

It is difficult to discuss the keyboard and display separately, because they operate as a unit. This combination, in fact, has a name: *video terminal*. The reason we mention the combination is that it has special features, especially if you are used to a standard typewriter.

First, the video display does not provide a permanent record (or *hard copy*) of what it shows. Of course, this is often a blessing, since it saves paper and keeps the operation nice and clean. However, sometimes, as in bookkeeping or accounting, you simply must have a permanent record. Besides, you will find it awkward to carry the display around for consultation and you cannot mail it to someone. The lack of a permanent record of your work creates new problems. A printer is part of the solution, but you will have to practice a little to become accustomed to this new way of working.

Second, the video display has a limited area. It lets you see only a certain amount (sometimes called a *window*) of material at any one time.

What happens when the computer fills the screen? After it prints on the bottom line, it automatically moves the entire screen up one line to make room for another line. When that happens, the top line is lost from view. This movement is called *scrolling*, since it is like unfolding or rolling up an ancient scroll.

Third, a video display simply has characteristics different from those of a typewriter. Obviously, erasing characters is much simpler, since no permanent record has been made. Similarly, you can move entire lines or sections up or down more easily and much faster on a screen than on paper. After all, the video display can do everything that a television can do, and at the same speed.

The new characteristics and freedom of the video display require additional control keys and markers. In the first place, how do you know where you are working on the screen? On a typewriter, you can see where the carriage or typing mechanism is; on the screen, there is nothing to see. Computers solve this problem by providing a special marker or *cursor* that indicates the current position. On the IBM PC, the cursor is a blinking underline.

Note the extent of freedom provided by a cursor on a video display. Unlike using a typewriter, you can rapidly move the cursor anywhere on the screen—up a line, down eight lines, all the way to the right or left. You make the cursor move by pressing the keys marked with arrows on the numeric keypad.

The up-arrow key (lowercase 8) moves the cursor up the screen; the down-arrow key (lowercase 2) moves the cursor down the screen; the left- and right-arrow keys (lowercase 4 and 6) move the cursor left or right on the current line. These four keys repeat automatically; as long as you hold them down, the cursor keeps moving. The action is immediate, too, since there are no mechanical parts. After you work with a keyboard and video display for a while, going back to a typewriter will seem like going from an automobile back to a horse and buggy.

Mass Storage Devices

Humans have "permanent" memory. Once you fully learn skills or facts, such as how to read and write or what year Columbus discovered America, they are embedded in your brain. They are not lost like a telephone number you dialed once or yesterday's news headlines.

By contrast, a computer develops amnesia the instant you switch off the power. That is, its memory is erased completely, and it forgets everything it ever knew.

Hence, if you (or a gremlin in the power line) switch off the power or pull the plug, all your current work will be lost. For this reason, computer users need a way to store data and programs, so that this information can be loaded back later into the computer's memory. We refer to the units that let users do this as *mass storage devices.*

The PC can employ two types of mass storage devices: cassette recorders and disk drives. Cassette recorders are inexpensive, but they are also slow, inconvenient to use, and somewhat unreliable. Therefore, most PC owners prefer disk storage, and we will generally assume that you have at least one disk drive.

Disk Drives. The PC can house two disk drives in a recess at the front of the computer. These are small black rectangular objects with a cross-shaped slot in front. Disk drives act much like record players except that they play thin, flexible disks called *floppy disks* (or sometimes just *disks* or *diskettes*). PC disks are $5\frac{1}{4}$ inches in diameter (roughly the size of a 45-rpm record) and come 10 to a box.

The PC refers to its disk drives as A and B. If you have two drives, A is the left-hand drive and B is the right-hand drive. If you have only one drive, it acts as both A and B. Generally, A is the main drive, and B is the secondary drive.

Comparing Disk Drives with Cassette Recorders. Like tape recorders, disk drives record information on a magnetic surface. But that is where the similarity ends.

To read something from a tape, a recorder must wind or rewind the tape until it reaches the correct position. If the item is close to where the recorder started, it will be reached quickly. Unfortunately, the item could just as easily be at the other end of the tape, so tape storage tends to be slow.

By contrast, the mechanism (or *head*) of a disk drive slides along an arm that extends radially across the disk's surface. Once the head is in the right position, it can read something as the surface location spins by. No winding is necessary, so this occurs much faster than is possible with tape.

Printers

To produce a written record of your results or programs, you must have a printer. The two most common types of printers are dot matrix and daisy wheel.

Dot matrix printers form characters by making patterns of dots in a rectangular grid. For example, the IBM 80 CPS Matrix Printer uses a 9-dot by 9-dot grid. Figure 1-2 shows how this printer constructs the letters K and j.

Dot matrix printers are generally fast and inexpensive. The 80-CPS Matrix Printer produces (as you might expect) 80 characters per second. This is about 1000 words per minute, 10 times the speed of the fastest typists.

Because of the gaps between the dots, the output of dot matrix printers is not as clear and readable as the output of a typewriter. Of course, the more dots in the printer's grid, the better its output looks, since the gaps are smaller. Dot matrix printers also have the advantage that they can produce plots and pictures since they can create any pattern of dots (say, for example, a rectangle) as opposed to being limited to printed characters.

By contrast, a *daisy wheel printer* works like a typewriter. That is, it actually imprints entire characters on the paper. Daisy wheel printers

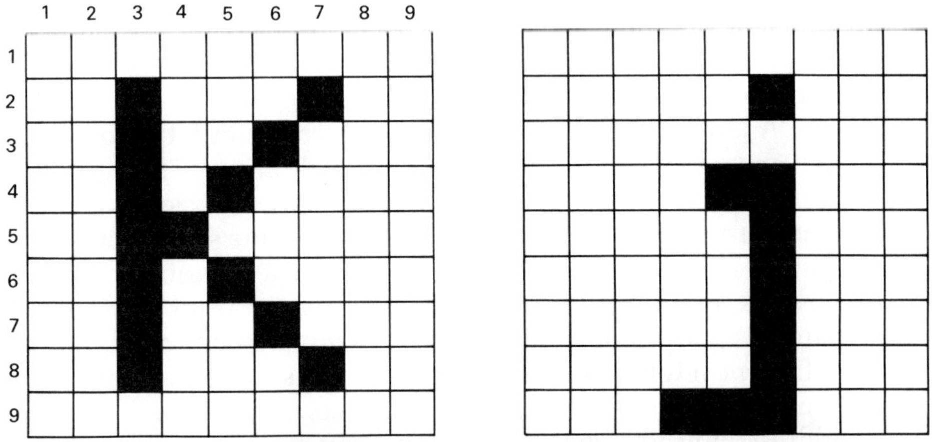

Figure 1-2. Typical dot matrix characters

obviously cannot draw pictures, but a user can obtain different typefaces and character sets (e.g., Greek letters or mathematical symbols) by changing character wheels. In general, daisy wheel printers are more expensive than dot matrix printers and are much slower.

Which type of printer should you buy? If you do not need letter-quality output, a dot matrix printer is the best choice because of its higher speed. But if you need typewriter-quality print for business letters or documents, you should invest in a daisy wheel printer. Better yet, if you can afford it, buy one of each!

Paddles and Joysticks

These devices are generally used to play computer games. A *paddle* is a box with a knob that looks like the volume control on a television set. Rotating the knob makes a game element—perhaps a spaceship or an athlete—move up, down, right, or left.

The control for a *joystick* is a small vertical rod like the stick shift in a sports car. This rod lets you move the game element in *two* dimensions (that is, horizontally and vertically) at the same time.

To add paddles or joysticks to your computer, you need an optional circuit board: the IBM *Game Control Adapter.* One Game Control Adapter can handle up to four paddles or two joysticks.

Modems

Modems are devices that let one computer talk to another over a telephone line. To add a modem, you need an optional circuit board: the *Asynchronous Communications Adapter.*

A modem is necessary to use electronic bulletin boards or information services such as CompuServe, Dow Jones, or The Source. Electronic bulletin boards allow subscribers to advertise goods and services to other subscribers via computer. For a one-time subscription charge, plus a modest hourly fee (a few dollars) and telephone costs, information services provide stock market quotations, the front pages of major newspapers, sports scores, restaurant and hotel recommendations, and even entire encyclopedias. Like bulletin boards, information services also let you send messages to other subscribers. Your dealer probably has the address of at least one information service.

Light Pens

A light pen resembles a standard writing pen that is connected to a computer by a wire. Touching the light pen to the screen and pressing a button tells the computer to do something at that particular screen position, such as draw a line from the last position, move an object there, or select the answer on that line. Thus, light pens are convenient for drawing pictures on the screen and also make it easy for nontypists (e.g., children or disabled people) to answer questions or enter information.

1.2 SOFTWARE

IBM provides three programs with the PC. Two (Cassette BASIC and Basic Input/Output System) are built into the computer, while the third (Diagnostics) comes on a disk or cassette.

Because the PC is so popular, many companies besides IBM have written programs for it. Given enough time, there will certainly be PC programs for every imaginable field, from accounting to zoology. Most outside programs come on disk rather than on cassette. We will discuss the included programs first and then survey the other software.

BASIC

Human beings can communicate with computers just as they communicate with each other: through an established language. Computer scientists have devised many languages for use with computers. Like human languages, computer languages may be primitive or advanced. Some are designed for specific applications, such as drawing pictures, solving equations, or producing business forms. Like human languages, each computer language has its own fans and critics and its own personality. Think of how the sounds of French, German, and Russian, for instance, each affect you differently.

The most popular computer language for small computers is appropriately called BASIC (*B*eginners *A*ll-Purpose *S*ymbolic *I*nstruction *C*ode). BASIC uses English-like words and phrases, making it easy to learn and use.

To make a computer do something, such as prepare paychecks or teach a student about fractions, you must combine BASIC instructions in the proper sequence. The sequence of instructions is called a *program*. Chapter 3 covers BASIC in more detail.

The PC has a built-in BASIC called *Cassette BASIC*. This program reads the BASIC commands you enter and makes the computer do what you want.

Basic Input/Output System (BIOS)

IBM calls the internal program that controls the PC's overall operation the *Basic Input/Output System* or BIOS. (Input/output is a common computer term. Input is simply what goes into the computer and output is what comes out of it.) The BIOS interprets words typed in from the keyboard, displays characters on the screen, and transfers data to and from the disk drives, printer, and whatever else is attached to the computer.

In short, without BIOS, the PC would be just a collection of metal, plastic, and electrical circuits. BIOS is the PC's native intelligence that makes it a computer.

As you might expect, BIOS is a large, complex program. Only an experienced computer programmer can fully understand it. Fortunately, most PC users do not need to know how BIOS works; we mention it here only to let you know what the term means.

Diagnostics

The third program, *Diagnostics*, is not built-in, but comes on a disk or cassette. Diagnostics tests the computer, keyboard, display, and printer to help you identify and isolate operating problems. The idea here is to reduce how much of the computer you have to take to your dealer for repair.

Business Programs

Many PC programs serve business needs, such as inventory, billing, bookkeeping, payroll, tax accounting, and maintenance of personnel and customer records. Without a doubt, the most popular business program is the *electronic spreadsheet*, a new type of program that originated with personal computers.

Electronic Spreadsheets. To explain what an electronic spreadsheet does, let us consider a practical application. Suppose that you own a clothing store and want to find out how your business is doing. You could take a large piece of paper and rule it off into rows and columns. Each row would correspond to a different department: men's suits, children's wear, sportswear, women's fashions, and so on.

The first 12 columns would be monthly sales totals, followed by yearly totals, comparisons with previous months or previous years, commissions, sales taxes, and so forth. You would probably want to add down the columns (giving totals for a particular month) and also across the rows (giving annual totals for a particular department). You might also want to figure total receipts, net profits (receipts minus costs), and other numbers.

How would you do this by hand? You would take out your calculator, enter the numbers from your account books, and produce one result after another. Surely this would be a long, tedious, error-prone task. The electronic spreadsheet, however, lets you label rows and columns on the screen and tell the computer how they are related.

For example, you could mark columns for each month and say that the yearly total column is the sum of the 12 monthly columns. Similarly, you could say that the monthly total row is the sum of all departmental totals for a particular month. You then enter your data, and the computer quickly and automatically performs all the calculations at once. It is like having many calculators, each set up to do a specific task.

Furthermore, if you enter a sales figure incorrectly, you can change it, and the computer will instantly recalculate everything. Electronic spreadsheets can obviously save time for an accountant, banker, insurance agent, purchasing manager, sales manager, broker, or anyone else who works with figures. Programs such as VisiCalc, SuperCalc, CalcStar, and Multiplan are as great a convenience as the inexpensive pocket calculator.

Educational Programs

For educators and parents, there are educational programs that can teach children arithmetic, languages, history, geography, and other subjects. There are also adult education programs that teach typing, computer programming, and other skills.

Word Processors

For writers, secretaries, or anyone else who writes reports or letters, there are word processors and spelling checkers. A word processor lets the user display text on the screen, correct it, change it, and even move words and paragraphs around without committing anything to paper. Popular word processors include WordStar, Volkswriter, Perfect Writer, and EasyWriter. These programs are particularly handy for producing form letters, creating legal documents from standard paragraphs, and developing new proposals or reports from previous work.

A spelling checker, such as SpellStar or The Word Plus, checks for spelling errors in a letter or report produced with a word processor. It does this by comparing each word in the document against its built-in dictionary. If it finds words that are not in its dictionary, it displays them on the screen, one by one. The user must then tell the spelling checker whether to correct the word, ignore it (e.g., it is a proper name or part of a book title), or add it to the dictionary (e.g., it is a technical term not found in most dictionaries).

Entertainment Programs

Although the PC is not primarily intended for playing games, many games are available for it. These include space games, war games, adventure and fantasy games, and others whose names are more familiar to a 10-year-old than to a middle-aged author.

Operating Systems

If your PC has a disk drive, you will need IBM's *Disk Operating System*, or DOS (rhymes with "boss"). DOS is a collection of programs that makes it possible to move information to and from the disk. Thus, DOS acts as the computer's chief administrative officer. We will describe DOS in more detail in Chapter 4.

The IBM DOS (called PC-DOS) is not the only disk operating system you can buy. Another popular one is *CP/M-86*, a product of Digital Research, Inc., of Pacific Grove, California. CP/M-86 is a version of the widely used CP/M operating system. Thousands of programs depend on (or *run under*) CP/M. CP/M-86 makes many of these programs usable on the PC.

Disk BASICs

The IBM DOS disk also includes two versions of BASIC intended specifically for disk systems. One is (cleverly) called Disk BASIC; the other is called Advanced BASIC. These are simply dialects of BASIC (much like dialects of human languages); they differ only in details, which we will discuss in Chapter 3.

Other Computer Languages

Finally, you may have applications for which BASIC is not well suited. Using BASIC could then be like trying to describe pasta making in Swahili or a tropical rain forest in Russian. You might consider using some other computer language for these applications. Popular alternatives to BASIC include C, COBOL (*Co*mmon *B*usiness-*O*riented *L*anguage), Forth, FORTRAN (*For*mula *Tran*slation), Pascal, and assembly language.

Writing Your Own Programs

Of course, sometimes you simply cannot find a program that solves your problem, much as you may not be able to find a book on a specific subject. If the problem is large, such as keeping school attendance records or tracking commodities markets, you should probably wait for a program you can buy. However, if the problem is simple, such as calculating a loan payment or converting foreign sales from francs to dollars, you may want to write your own program.

Developing a computer program involves the same thought processes as building a dog house, preparing a tax return, or writing a book report. That is, you must decide what to do, get the right tools, and *do it.* Chapter 3 has more to say about writing BASIC programs.

In fact, most computer users buy more programs than they write, and many never write any programs at all. Writing programs is not terribly difficult, but it is time consuming, just like writing magazine articles or book reports. We do not want to discourage you from programming; it is a fascinating challenge and one that you are likely to enjoy. At the same time, you can use a computer productively without writing any of your own programs, much as you can be a musician without composing music or an actor without writing scripts.

Chapter 2

GETTING STARTED

Now that you know something about the PC's hardware and software, you can begin using it. This chapter explains how to load the Disk Operating System (DOS), enter the date and time, determine what is on your disk, load BASIC, and run programs. In short, you will learn everything needed to start working with your computer. A final section discusses procedures you should follow when operating your PC.

2.1 LOADING DOS

If you have a disk drive, you must start by placing the IBM DOS disk in drive A before turning on the power. Remember, A is the left-hand drive if you have two drives. To place a disk in a drive, gently raise the drive door (a small, black piece of plastic in the upper middle of the drive). *Don't let the door spring open* or you might jar something loose. The door should catch at the top so it is out of the way. Now remove the DOS disk from its envelope and insert it into the drive slot, label side up with the label toward you (see Figure 2-1).

Applying even pressure, slide the disk into the drive until it stops.

Figure 2-1. The correct way to insert a disk

Do not force it. Now press down on the drive door until it latches closed. If you feel some resistance from the disk, remove it and try again.

With the DOS disk in drive A, you are ready to turn on the power. Power is controlled by the large red switch near the back of the computer, on the right-hand side. Flip this switch to its On position.

You won't hear anything immediately, because the PC first runs a test program that checks to be sure that everything is working. However, within 15 or 20 seconds you should hear the computer beep and the disk drive make grinding sounds. This means that the PC is putting DOS into its memory (we call this *loading* DOS). The red light on the drive should go on at this time, too. If nothing happens, check your power cord connection.

Entering the Date and Time

When the drive stops and the red light goes off, the screen should show the message

```
Current date is Tue 1-01-1980
Enter new date:
```

followed by the cursor. If you do not see the message, turn the Brightness and Contrast knobs on your display clockwise.

Now enter the date in the form day-month-year. For example, if the date is October 8, 1983, you should type **10-8-83** and press Enter (the key with the bent arrow). The computer will now display

```
Current time is 0:03:56.39
Enter new time:
```

This current time, like the preceding current date, is a value that the PC gets set to unless you change it. Don't bother setting the time for now; just press Enter.

When you press Enter, the PC displays

```
The IBM Personal Computer DOS
Version x.xx (C)Copyright IBM Corp 198x

A>_
```

This message tells you that you have successfully loaded DOS into your computer. It is now awaiting your next command; the A⟩ tells you that drive A is active.

Finding What's on the Disk

The next step is to find out which programs your disk contains. To do this, type **DIR** (directory) and press Enter.

The screen should show a long list of words, abbreviations, and numbers. Unfortunately, they will move by (*scroll*) so quickly that you will not be able to read them. However, you can stop the scrolling at any time. Simply hold down the Ctrl key (just left of A) and press Scroll Lock (upper right-hand corner of the keyboard). In fact, you can press Num Lock instead of Scroll Lock; it works the same way, except that Num Lock allows you to resume scrolling by pressing the space bar.

Each line in the directory tells you four things about a program on the disk: its name, whether it is a BASIC program (BAS) or a DOS command program (COM), its length in bytes, and the date it was put on the disk.

IBM has provided an interesting assortment of demonstration programs on the DOS disk. Some play tunes over the computer's built-in speaker, others draw pictures on the screen, and one calculates mortgage amortization schedules. However, because these programs are written in BASIC, you must prepare the computer for BASIC before you can run them.

2.2 STARTING BASIC

You prepare the computer to accept BASIC programs by typing **BASIC** (or **basic**, the computer will accept either) and then pressing Enter. When the computer has finished placing BASIC in its memory, the screen will show the message

```
The IBM Personal Computer Basic
Version Dx.xx Copyright IBM Corp. 198x

xxxxx Bytes free
Ok
```

where xxxxx is a five-digit number that shows how many bytes (characters) in memory are available to you. It seems like a very large number now, but it will become smaller as you continue to use the computer.

The final line, *Ok*, is the computer's way of telling you that BASIC is ready for you to enter something. You will see many Oks if you do much BASIC programming.

The words numbered 1 through 0 at the bottom of the screen tell you what function keys F1 through F10 do. For example, *1 LIST* tells you that pressing F1 makes the computer display (list) its current BASIC program on the screen.

Running a BASIC Program

To show how to actually run a program, let us use a demonstration program from the DOS disk. (The terms *running* or *executing* a program simply mean making the computer perform the series of instructions.) A good first choice is the program SAMPLES, which simply lists the demonstration programs.

To run a program from the disk,

1. Type **RUN**.
2. Press the space bar, then type a quotation mark (") and the program's name (for example, **"SAMPLES**).
3. Press Enter.

If you do this, the screen should show a title page for the SAMPLES program. To get to the actual program, press the space bar.

Now the screen shows a selection (*menu*) of programs you can run by pressing keys A through J; see Figure 2-2. In addition to the program's

```
SAMPLE PROGRAMS

A—MUSIC        (32k)
B—ART          (32k-Color/Graphics)
C—MORTGAGE     (48k)
D—CIRCLE       (BASICA-Color/Graphics)
E—DONKEY       (BASICA-Color/Graphics)
F—PIECHART     (BASICA-Color/Graphics)
G—BALL         (BASICA-Color/Graphics)
H—COLORBAR     (32k)
I—CALENDAR     (32k)
J—SPACE        (BASICA-Color/Graphics)
ESC KEY—EXIT

ENTER LETTER OF PROGRAM

NOTE: All of the above programs require 48k if using BASICA
```

Figure 2-2. Menu for the SAMPLES program

selection letter and its name, the menu tells you what equipment you need to run it. In particular, it tells you

1. How much memory your computer must have, either 32K or 48K.
2. Which version of BASIC is required. BASIC refers to the Disk BASIC we are currently running; BASICA refers to Advanced BASIC, which is only slightly different from Disk BASIC. Programs marked BASICA can only be run if you type **BASICA** rather than **BASIC** in response to the A⟩ prompt.
3. What kind of display you must have. *Color/Graphics* indicates that your computer must have a color display, a television set, or a television monitor.

If you attempt to run a program without the proper amount of memory, active version of BASIC, or proper display, the PC will issue a polite, but curt, error message.

An Example Program—Computer Music. An entertaining program to try from SAMPLES' menu is MUSIC, which plays tunes through the PC's built-in speaker. To run MUSIC, press the A key. When the title page appears, press the space bar to display MUSIC's menu.

MUSIC gives you a choice of 11 different tunes, which you select by pressing A through K. Indulge yourself! Try as many tunes as you want. When you are tired of the music, press the Esc (escape) key, which is next to the 1 key on the typewriter part of the keyboard. Esc will return you to the SAMPLES menu. You may then want to try some other programs to give yourself more practice in operating the PC.

2.3 SUMMARY OF START-UP PROCEDURE

We may summarize the procedure for starting up your PC as follows:

1. Load DOS. Put the DOS disk in drive A, turn on the power, and enter the date and time when requested.
2. Type **DIR** to see what programs are on your disk.
3. Type **BASIC** to prepare your computer for accepting BASIC programs.
4. Type **RUN "PNAME** to load program PNAME into memory and have the computer execute it.

2.4 OPERATING YOUR PC

Now that you know how to start up your PC, we should say some things about how to operate it properly. In general, operating a computer is not much more difficult than operating an automobile or a home entertainment center. You need not be a programmer or an electrical wizard. PCs will operate in everyday settings with a minimum of special attention, but a normal amount of care and caution will help to avoid any problems.

Setting up the Computer

A PC does not require any special environment. It can be placed on any convenient desk or table that will support a standard office typewriter. Since the PC is grounded, you are in no danger of electrical shock. You should, however, arrange the cables and power cord so that no one can trip over them or inadvertently yank them out.

Be sure to provide proper lighting for your video display. If you have never used one before, you may encounter some eyestrain. Experiment with the lighting until the setup seems reasonable.

The printer is the only unit that needs solid support. If you put it on a flimsy table, it will "dance" around while printing. This not only makes it noisy, but it could loosen internal parts. A special printer stand or a heavy desk or table will provide the required support. If you still find the printer noisy (daisy wheel printers often are), you might consider buying an acoustical cover for it.

Other minor accessories you might consider include plastic dust covers (available from many sources) and a power line filter that keeps electrical noise (such as that produced by vacuum cleaners and power tools) from interfering with the computer. You will probably also want to buy disk holders and a book rack for manuals and other documentation.

Working with Disks

The major operating procedures you must learn involve working with floppy disks. You must, for example, be sure that you have a backup copy of each important disk. You should not use the original copies of disks like the DOS disk. Instead, you should make a backup copy, then file the original in a safe place, and use the backup copy in your everyday work. Appendix A tells you how to make a backup copy of a disk.

Formatting Disks. Many programs require that you prepare or *format* blank disks before using them. You can think of formatting as "breaking in" the disk, just as you break in a new baseball glove or pair of shoes. Appendix A tells you how to format a disk.

Handling and Storing Disks. High-quality disks are often guaranteed for five years. They should last at least that long if you take a few simple precautions, such as the following:

- Never touch the exposed recording surfaces. The perspiration on your fingers may destroy data.
- Always return a disk to its envelope as soon as you are through with it. Even minute debris could damage the disk.
- Don't bend or (heaven forbid) fold a disk.
- Keep the computer area clean. Avoid heat, moisture, and dust.
- Insert disks into the drive carefully. Don't force them, and never force the door shut.
- Keep disks away from magnetic devices. Never lay a disk on top of your display or on a telephone.
- Use only a felt-tipped pen to write on disk labels. A ball-point pen could damage the recording surface.

When storing disks, take the following precautions:

- Label them so you know what they contain. Otherwise, you will have to load each one into the computer to obtain a directory.

- Put them in protective envelopes and store them upright in a covered box.
- Keep them in a place where the humidity is never higher than 80 percent or lower than 8 percent and where the temperature is never higher than 109°F (43°C) or lower than 39°F (4°C).
- Keep them away from cigarette smoke. If you must smoke, do it in another room.
- Keep them out of direct sunlight.

Printer Care

The printer requires some special care, too. To operate your printer with minimum inconvenience, you must

- Insert paper carefully. Be sure that it is aligned properly, both at the sides and at the top. Never force paper in or out.
- Keep the output from piling up or blocking the flow of paper. A paper holder or basket may be a good investment.
- Never drop anything into the mechanism, put your hands into the printer while it is operating, or change anything while the printer is on.
- Follow your printer manual when inserting paper, changing the ribbon, or cleaning the printer. Many repair services sell regular maintenance contracts that ensure proper attention to minor problems.

Keyboard and Display Care

A keyboard and video display require the same care as a typewriter and television set. As for the keyboard, you should keep it clean, cover it when it is not in use, and avoid spilling liquids on it. When typing, stroke it as gently as possible; don't pound on it as though it were a manual typewriter.

As for the video display, clean the screen regularly with a soft cloth and liquid glass cleaner. Don't leave it on for long periods of time with only the cursor displayed.

Computer Care

The computer itself is the most carefree part of your system. About all you need to do is leave it alone and avoid blocking its vents.

Chapter 3

BASIC

BASIC is a language that allows people to talk to computers. Like Spanish or English, BASIC consists of words and phrases with concise meanings. When properly combined (into what we call a *program*), these words and phrases provide the computer with an ordered list of instructions to follow.

This chapter introduces BASIC and provides the information you need to write simple programs. Books that teach BASIC programming for the PC in more detail include

- Goldstein, Larry Joel, and Martin Goldstein. *The IBM Personal Computer: An Introduction to Programming and Applications.* Bowie, Md.: Robert J. Brady/Prentice-Hall, 1982.
- Lien, David A., *Learning IBM BASIC for the Personal Computer.* San Diego, Calif.: CompuSoft, 1982.

We will describe only the commonly used features of BASIC. We have, however, included several tables that list less common features. Since BASIC has many options, we have indicated them with brackets.

You should not actually type the brackets; they merely signify that the characters inside them are optional.

3.1 ENTERING AND EDITING BASIC PROGRAMS

Chapter 2 described how to load BASIC. We will now discuss how to actually enter programs, change them, run them, and transfer them to and from disks.

Operating Modes

Once you have loaded BASIC, you can operate in either the *command mode* or the *program mode*. In the command mode, the computer does what it is told immediately. In the more common program mode, the computer saves a series of instructions in its memory for later execution. IBM's BASIC manual refers to the command mode as the *direct mode* and the program mode as the *indirect mode*.

Command Mode. In the command mode, the PC acts like an expensive calculator. When you type an instruction (or *command*) and press Enter, the computer does what you tell it to do and then forgets the instruction. To see the result on the screen, you must first type **PRINT**, then the instruction. (Again, you may use upper- or lowercase, so **print** works just as well.)

For example, to add 19 to 24 and display (print) the sum, type **PRINT 19+24** (followed, as usual, by Enter). On the screen, you will see

```
Ok
PRINT 19+24 (press Enter)
 43
Ok
```

We have placed what the computer puts on the screen in regular type and what you enter in **boldface** type.

Program Mode. While the command mode is occasionally convenient, an inexpensive calculator can perform simple arithmetic as well as the PC can. The computer's advantage over the calculator is its ability to remember a series of instructions—a recipe, if you will—and perform that series whenever you want.

We described a program as a series of instructions. The individual instructions that make up a program are referred to as *statements*. In the program mode, the computer saves the BASIC statements you type in its memory. Then, when you type the command **RUN**, it performs (or *executes*) the stored statements.

Line Numbers

How does the computer know whether to save statements or execute them immediately? The answer is that you must *number* the lines that the computer should save. For example, the sequence

```
Ok
10 PRINT 19+24 (press Enter)
RUN            (press Enter)
 43
Ok
```

gives the same result as our earlier example of the command mode. However, now the computer keeps **PRINT 19+24** in its memory and will execute it again if you type **RUN**. Generally, we use the program mode to enter statements into memory and the command mode to tell the computer what to do with the program (for example, run it or save it on disk).

Hence, *a BASIC program is simply a series of numbered statements*. The line numbers tell the computer how to order the statements in its memory. When you type **RUN**, the computer starts with the lowest-numbered statement and proceeds in numerical order unless told to do otherwise.

Line numbers may be up to five digits long, from 1 to 99999. You may enter lines in any order you want since BASIC automatically puts them in numerical order. Programmers generally prefer to use a simple, regular spacing such as 10, 20, 30, 40, and so on. The gaps between line numbers allow the programmer to add new lines at any point.

BASIC Commands

Commands tell BASIC to do something to a program in memory or on a disk (a disk *file*). Do not confuse commands with *statements*, which are instructions for the computer, not for BASIC. In the remainder of this section, we will discuss the common BASIC commands listed in Table 3-1.

Editing a Program

All computer users occasionally make mistakes entering programs. Fortunately, most mistakes are easy to correct on the PC.

TABLE 3-1. COMMON BASIC COMMANDS*

Command	*Action*
DELETE start[-end]	Deletes program lines.
EDIT line	Displays a line for editing.
FILES	Displays the names of files on a disk.
KILL"filename.BAS"	Erases a program from a disk.
LIST [start][-end]	Lists on the screen the program currently in memory.
LLIST [start][-end]	Lists on the printer the program currently in memory.
LOAD "filename	Loads a program from disk into memory.
NAME "oldname AS "newname	Renames a disk file.
NEW	Erases the program currently in memory.
RUN	Executes the program currently in memory.
RUN "filename	Executes a program stored on a disk.
SAVE "filename	Gives the current program a name and saves it on disk.
TROFF	Turns trace off.
TRON	Turns trace on.

* Brackets indicate that the item(s) inside them are optional.

Replacing, Inserting, and Deleting Lines. If you type something incorrectly, simply re-enter the line number and retype the line. BASIC will automatically replace the old line. Typing a new line 10, for example, makes BASIC forget the old line 10.

If you accidentally omit a line completely, you can add it at any time by typing it with the appropriate line number. To delete a line entirely, simply type its number and then press Enter.

A shorthand way of deleting several lines at once is to use the DELETE command, which takes the form

```
DELETE start-end
```

where *start* and *end* are line numbers. For example, DELETE 10-100 erases lines starting with 10 and finishing with 100.

Editing Lines. IBM BASIC lets you add, replace, and delete portions of lines, using specially designated keys. Generally, these are the lowercase keys on the numeric keypad.

Table 3-2 summarizes the keys you can use to edit BASIC programs. They fall into three groups: cursor-moving keys (all editing takes place at the cursor position), mode control keys, and character-editing keys. When the Ctrl (control) key is mentioned, you must hold it down

TABLE 3-2. SCREEN EDITING KEYS

Key(s)	*Action*
	Cursor-Moving Keys
Home	(Numeric keypad 7) Moves the cursor to the upper left-hand corner of the screen.
Ctrl Home	Clears the screen and moves the cursor to the upper left-hand corner of the screen.
↑	(Numeric keypad 8) Moves the cursor up one line.
↓	(Numeric keypad 2) Moves the cursor down one line.
←	(Numeric keypad 4) Moves the cursor left one position.
→	(Numeric keypad 6) Moves the cursor right one position.
Ctrl →	Moves the cursor right to the next word.
Ctrl ←	Moves the cursor left to the preceding word.
End	(Numeric keypad 1) Moves the cursor to the end of the current line.
→|	Moves the cursor to the next tab stop.
	Mode Control Keys
Ins	(Numeric keypad 0) Turns Insert Mode on if it is off, or off if it is on. *When Insert Mode is on*, newly typed characters are inserted just ahead of the cursor. *When Insert Mode is off*, newly typed characters replace existing characters.
Ctrl Break	Returns BASIC to the command mode, without saving any changes that were made to the current line.
	Character-Editing Keys
Del	(Numeric keypad decimal point) Deletes character at the current cursor position.
←	(Key to the left of Num Lock) Deletes character to the left of the cursor.
Ctrl End	Erases all characters to the end of the line, starting at the cursor position.
Esc	Erases the line from the screen, but not from memory.

while pressing the other key. For example, to get Ctrl Break (stop a program and return control to the user), press Ctrl *first* and hold it down, *then* press Break. Break, by the way, is in the top right-hand corner; it is the same key as Scroll Lock (the word Break is printed on the front).

Listing a Program

After entering a program, you should examine it to make sure that it is correct. To show a program on the screen, you can either type **LIST** or press F1, followed by Enter. (Note that the PC tells you what the function keys mean on the bottom line of the screen.) If you spot a mistake in the listing, use the editing keys to move the cursor to it and then correct the mistake.

LIST Command. LIST has other useful forms as well. As you might imagine, listing a long program on the screen is awkward since there is not enough room to show it all. Lines fly by, and it is difficult to stop the scrolling to see a particular section. However, LIST can display part of a program if you include starting and ending line numbers. It takes the form

```
LIST start-end
```

where *start* and *end* are line numbers.

You can even omit start or end if you want to list a single line, everything after start, or everything up to and including end. Some examples are:

LIST 200-280 lists all lines between 200 and 280.

LIST 200 lists just line 200.

LIST 200- lists 200 and all lines that follow it.

LIST -280 lists all lines from the beginning through 280.

LLIST Command. You can obtain a printed listing by turning on your printer, switching it to *on-line*, and typing **LLIST**. Note the extra L here; be careful to distinguish between LIST (for the screen) and LLIST (for the printer).

Running a Program

When you have corrected your mistakes, you can see whether the program does what you want by running it. To run a program you can either type **RUN** or press F2, followed by Enter.

Finding an Error. Unfortunately, programs do not always do what you expect. Like some popular cartoon characters, the computer always takes you literally; it does *exactly* what you tell it to do, no more and no less. In fact, only occasionally does a program work perfectly the first time. Most of the time, the program does something slightly wrong (such as printing four numbers instead of five), halts and displays an error message, or simply runs endlessly.

If the program does not run perfectly, you must find the problem and fix it. In computer jargon, you must *debug* the program.

Trace. One approach to debugging a program is simply to obtain more information about what it is doing. The additional information will often make the error obvious. For example, if you turn the *trace* on, the PC will list in order each line number it executes. This list should show you where the computer is being misled or stuck.

To turn on the trace, type **TRON** or press the F7 key and then type **RUN**. To turn off the trace, type **TROFF** or press the F8 key. TRON and TROFF have useful variations. You can trace a selected set of lines, rather than an entire program, by inserting TRON and TROFF as numbered lines. For example, to trace between lines 100 and 500, you could insert **99 TRON** and **501 TROFF** in your program before running it.

Saving a Program on Disk

As we mentioned earlier, computers forget everything when you switch off the power. To avoid having to retype programs every time you want to run them, you should save them on disk. Before you can store a program on a disk, you must *format* the disk as described in Appendix A.

File Names. We refer to programs and data stored on disk as *files*. On the PC, each disk can hold up to 64 files. Each file must have a unique name; the name can consist of up to eight letters (upper- or lowercase), digits, or the symbols $ and @.

Of course, programmers generally try to make the names meaningful (such as PAYROLL, ENGINE6, or ROT180) and easy to distinguish and type. You should avoid names that are very similar (such as XXX and XXXX) or difficult to type (such as A0O0 or I1I1). Be careful about the usual confusion between 0 (zero) and O (uppercase letter O) and between 1 (one) and I (uppercase letter I). Z and 2 and S and 5 are also sometimes hard to differentiate.

SAVE Command. The SAVE command allows you to save a BASIC program on disk. This command takes the form

```
SAVE "filename
```

where *filename* is the name you give your program. Note the quotation mark after SAVE; if you omit it, you will get an error message.

This simple form saves the program on the currently active drive. If you want to use the other drive, type its letter (**A** or **B**) and **:** (colon) before **filename**. The drive name combined with the filename is called a *filespec*. For example, if A is the active drive,

```
SAVE "LOANPAY
```

saves program LOANPAY on drive A and

```
SAVE "B:LOANPAY
```

saves program LOANPAY on drive B.

You can press the F4 key instead of typing **SAVE "**, in which case, F4 supplies the quotation mark automatically.

Loading a Program from Disk

To load a program from disk into memory, enter

```
LOAD "filename
```

(or **LOAD "B:filename**). You can press F3 instead of typing **LOAD "**. Here, again, the function key supplies the quotation mark automatically.

You can also run a program stored on disk directly. The command

```
RUN "filename
```

makes the computer both load the program into memory and execute it. Be careful, however. You cannot press F2 here instead of typing **RUN**, because F2 assumes that the program is already in memory.

Other BASIC Commands

NEW Command. NEW works like an eraser; it clears the entire memory, thereby preparing the computer to accept a new program. Use NEW carefully. On the one hand, be sure that you have SAVEd any programs you might need before typing **NEW**. On the other hand, be sure to type **NEW** before starting an entirely new program. If you do not, the lines you enter will be added to the existing program.

FILES Command. FILES is the BASIC equivalent of the DOS command DIR. Be sure you use the correct command to see what is on the disk. If you are in DOS, type **DIR**, but if you are in BASIC, type **FILES**. You can compare the differences between being in DOS and

TABLE 3-3. FUNCTION KEY ASSIGNMENTS*

Key	*Screen Label*	*Operation*
F1	LIST	Lists the BASIC program currently in memory.
F2	RUN	Executes the BASIC program currently in memory.
F3	LOAD "	Used in the form LOAD "*[drive:]filename* to read the program *filename* into memory from *drive:*.
F4	SAVE "	Used in the form SAVE "*[drive:]filename* to transfer the program in memory onto the disk in *drive:* and assign it the name *filename.*
F5	CONT	Directs BASIC to resume executing a program following Ctrl Break or a STOP or END statement.
F6	,"LPT1:"	Used after LIST (F1) to list a program on the printer.
F7	TRON	Turns on the trace feature.
F8	TROFF	Turns off the trace feature.
F9	KEY	Provides four options: ● *KEY* **OFF** erases the function key list on line 25. ● *KEY* **ON** reinstates the function key list on line 25. ● *KEY* **LIST** lists the current function key assignments. ● *KEY* **n,"text"** reassigns the function *text* to key F*n.*
F10	SCREEN	Reinitializes the screen to all text, in black and white.

* Brackets indicate that the item(s) inside them are optional.

being in BASIC to the differences between operating an automobile in the United States and in the United Kingdom; different laws and procedures apply in different places.

KILL Command. KILL erases a program from the disk. It takes the form

```
KILL "filename.BAS"
```

where *.BAS*" after the filename indicates a BASIC program.

Common uses of KILL are to erase old versions of programs and to delete programs when a disk is too full to accept the current program. If you try to SAVE a program on a full disk, the PC displays the error message *Disk full.* When that happens, you may either KILL a disk program (type **FILES** first if you don't remember what programs you have) or insert a new disk.

Function Keys

Table 3-3 summarizes the standard assignments for the PC's function keys. F9 lets you control the PC's function key list or assign the function keys to do whatever you want. When you press F9, the screen will display *KEY*. You can then supply one of four items:

1. KEY **OFF** to erase the function key list on line 25.
2. KEY **ON** to restore the function key list.
3. KEY **LIST** to display the current list.
4. A *function key number* followed by a command in quotation marks to assign a key to produce that command. If, for example, you want key F7 to enter PRINT into the computer, type

```
KEY 7,"PRINT"
```

3.2 INTRODUCTION TO BASIC PROGRAMMING

As we noted earlier, a program is a sequence of instructions that makes the computer do what you want. Hence, a programmer must decide what the computer should do, select instructions (*statements* in BASIC) that do the job, and combine them into a program.

Variables

The concept of a variable is often difficult for beginners. It brings back distant memories of X's and Y's and struggles with high school algebra. However, a variable is just a shorthand way of designating something that could have any of a number of values.

For instance, a person's age could be any number from 0 to 150 (excluding Methuselah); we can refer to it in general as a variable called AGE. This is simply more convenient than writing something like "the age of the person whose insurance premium is being calculated." We may also refer to *string variables*, such as a person's name (NAME$) or job classification (JCLASS$). At any particular time, AGE, NAME$, and JCLASS$ have specific values (for example, 37, Joe Smith, and welder), but those values change when we move on to the next person (for example, 53, Susan Jones, and mechanic).

Note the differences between numerical variables and string variables. Numerical variables such as AGE, WEIGHT, and HEIGHT have numerical values, whereas string variables such as NAME$, JCLASS$, and CITY$—the $ indicates "string"—have sequences of characters (*character strings*) as their values.

Variable Names. Variable names can be up to 40 characters long, although few programmers care to type that much. The first character must be a letter, whereas the rest can be letters, digits, or a decimal point. String variables must have names ending with a $.

Obviously, almost any name you can think of is acceptable to the computer. In general, programmers use the following criteria to select names:

1. The name should suggest its meaning or purpose. For example, you could choose W, WT, or WEIGHT for weight; MPH or MILES.PER.HOUR for speed; and PROFIT2Q or PROFIT.FOR.2ND.QUARTER for the second quarter's profit.
2. The name should be as short as possible, while still being reasonable. Thus, MPH is preferable to MILES.PER.HOUR, and CUR.YR is a reasonable abbreviation for CURRENT.YEAR.
3. The name should be easy to type without errors. The usual typing problems are several identical letters in a row (such as HHHHHHH), similar-looking characters (such as the letter O and the number 0, letter I and number 1, and letter S and number 5), and names that are similar to each other (such as XXXY and XXYX). There is no reason to invite typing errors; most of us make enough of them anyway.

Supervariables: Arrays

Variables can also represent groups of numbers or strings, such as the grades or names of students in a class, the ages or occupations of employees in a department, or the prices or descriptions of items in a grocery store. The common practice here is to give the entire group a name and refer to individual items by number or numbers. We generally refer to the entire group as an *array* and to the numbers that designate individual items as *indexes*.

For example, let us assume that we have a class of 40 students. We will arbitrarily assign them student numbers 1 through 40, just as a sports team assigns jersey numbers. Each student has a name (NAME$), a numerical grade (NGRADE), and a letter grade (LGRADE$).

We refer to a particular student by putting his or her student number in parentheses. That is, if George Brown is student 8, his name is NAME$(8), his numerical grade is NGRADE(8), and his letter grade is LGRADE$(8). Thus, poor George Brown has become just another number for a computer to digest. To find George's numerical grade, you simply tell the computer to **PRINT NGRADE(8)**. NAME$, NGRADE, and LGRADE$ are all arrays, while 8 is an index.

If the teacher has many classes, the array becomes more complicated. Now we need both a class number and a student number to identify a particular student. In this case, we put both numbers in the parentheses.

That is, if George Brown is in class 3 and is student 8, his name is NAME$(3,8), his numerical grade is NGRADE(3,8), and his letter grade is LGRADE$(3,8). We could even continue this process, assigning George to a particular department, school, campus, university system, and nation. This would result in one of the long series of identifying numbers—a hallmark of the computer age.

Setting up Arrays. BASIC has one special requirement for arrays: you must tell it how large they are. A program must contain a DIM (Dimension) statement for each array, declaring how large each index can be. Thus, a teacher with three classes of 40 students would specify

```
DIM NAME$(3,40), NGRADE(3,40), LGRADE$(3,40)
```

Programmers usually place DIM statements at the beginning of the program, where they are both easy to find and out of the way.

Computer Arithmetic

BASIC allows the arithmetic operations shown in Table 3-4. The operators +, −, and / (divide) are the same as in normal arithmetic, while * replaces × (multiply).

The operators \ and MOD divide integers (whole numbers), giving the quotient and remainder, respectively. For example, assume that EGGS = 40. EGGS\12 produces the quotient 3 (number of dozens) and EGGS MOD 12 produces the remainder 4 (eggs left over).

The operator ^ (uppercase symbol on the 6 key) raises a number to a power. Thus, 2^3 cubes 2 (i.e., 2 × 2 × 2), giving 8.

Parentheses in Arithmetic Expressions. Parentheses tell the computer what to do first. The computer always starts with whatever is

TABLE 3-4. ARITHMETIC OPERATORS

Operator	*Operation*	*Example*
+	Adds two values	SALES1Q+SALES2Q
−	Subtracts two values or Changes sign of a value	SALES−COSTS −BALANCE
*	Multiplies two values	TAXRATE*TOTAL
\	Divides two integers; gives quotient	INCHES\12
MOD	Divides two integers; gives remainder	INCHES MOD 12
/	Divides two nonintegers; gives quotient	MILES/HOURS
^	Raises value to a power	SIDE^3

inside the most parentheses. For example, *(A+B)/(C+D)* makes the computer add A to B, then add C to D, then divide A + B by C + D. *A+B/C+D*, on the other hand, gives the sum of B/C plus A plus D.

BASIC will accept as many parentheses as you want. When you use parentheses, however, be sure that *each left-hand parenthesis has a matching right-hand parenthesis*. Omitting a parenthesis will result in a *Syntax error* message.

3.3 STATEMENTS

We will describe BASIC's statements in two groups: those that programmers use most often (common statements) and those that they use less frequently (advanced statements).

Common Statements

Table 3-5 summarizes the statements that programmers use most often. We have divided them into 11 groups: print; data definition; repetition (looping); unconditional transfer; decision making; subroutine; keyboard input; data file; screen control; program terminating; and miscellaneous. Additional sound, graphics, and color statements are discussed in Chapter 5.

Print Statements. PRINT displays numbers or strings of characters on the screen.

When PRINTing, the computer divides the 80-character display line into five *zones* of 14 spaces each and one zone (at the far right) of 10 spaces. It prints the first item at the beginning of the first zone, the second item at the beginning of the next zone, and so on. For example,

```
10 PRINT 25.3, −16.7896, 3, .45
```

TABLE 3-5. COMMON STATEMENTS*

Statement	Action	Comments
	Print Statements	
LPRINT [expression(s)][;]	Prints expression(s) on printer.	Prints blank line if expressions are omitted.
PRINT [expression(s)][;]	Same as LPRINT, but displays expression(s) on screen. See also WRITE.	The symbol ? can be substituted for the word PRINT.
LPRINT USING ×$;expression(s)[;]	Prints expression(s) on printer, using format defined by ×$.	
PRINT USING ×$;expression(s)[;]	Same as LPRINT USING, but displays expression(s) on screen.	
WRITE [expression(s)]	Displays data on the screen.	Similar to PRINT, but WRITE puts comma between items and puts quotation marks around strings.
	Data Definition Statements	
DATA constant[, . .]	Sets up constants that are accessed by READ statements.	Constants can be numeric or string.
[LET] variable=expression	Assigns the value of an expression to a variable.	
READ variable[, . .]	Reads values from a DATA statement and assigns them to variables.	Variables may be numeric or string but must agree with DATA.
RESTORE [line]	Allows DATA statements to be reread.	
	Repetition Statement	
FOR variable = begin TO end [STEP n] . . . . NEXT [variable]	Executes the statements between FOR and NEXT a given number of times.	
	Unconditional Transfer Statement	
GOTO line	Jumps to a specified line.	
	Decision-Making Statements	
IF expression THEN clause [ELSE clause] or IF expression GOTO line [ELSE clause]	Makes a program flow decision based on the result returned by an expression.	If the expression is true, the THEN or GOTO clause is executed. Otherwise the next statement or the ELSE clause is executed.

* Brackets indicate that the item(s) inside them are optional.

TABLE 3-5. (continued)

Statement	Action	Comments
ON expression GOTO line[, . . .]	Jumps to one of several lines, based on the result returned by an expression.	If value of the expression is 0 or greater than number of lines in the list, computer continues to next statement.
	Subroutine Statements	
GOSUB line	Branches to a subroutine that starts at the specified line number.	A RETURN statement at the end of the subroutine returns computer to the statement that follows GOSUB.
ON expression GOSUB line[, . . .]	Same as ON . . . GOTO, but branches to a subroutine.	A RETURN statement at the end of the subroutine returns computer to the statement that follows ON . . . GOSUB.
	Keyboard Input Statement	
INPUT ["prompt string";]variable[, . . .]	Accepts variable values from the keyboard.	The optional prompt string display is followed with a question mark.
	Data File Statements	
CLOSE [filenum]	Concludes I/O to a file.	CLOSE alone (without file number) closes all OPENed files.
INPUT#filenum,variable[,variable . . .]	Reads data items from a file and assigns them to program variables.	
OPEN [drivename:]filename FOR INPUT AS [#]filenum OPEN [drivename:]filename FOR OUTPUT AS [#]filenum OPEN [drivename:]filename FOR APPEND AS [#]filenum	Allows a file to be accessed.	
PRINT #filenum,expression[,expression . . .]	Writes data to a file.	See also PRINT# USING.
PRINT #filenum,USING ×$;expression[,expression . . .]	Same as PRINT#, but writes the data using format defined by ×$.	For rules concerning ×$, see PRINT USING under *Print Statements.*
WRITE #filenum,expression[,expression . . .]	Similar to PRINT#, but WRITE# inserts commas between the items and encloses string with quotation marks.	
	Screen Control Statements	
CLS	Clears the screen.	
LOCATE [row][,col]	Moves the cursor to the specified row and column.	

TABLE 3-5. (continued)

Statement	*Action*	*Comments*
	Program-Terminating Statements	
END	Makes computer stop executing a program and closes all disk files.	
STOP	Same as END, but STOP does not close files.	
	Miscellaneous Statements	
MOTOR	Turns the cassette motor on if it is off, or off if it is on.	
REM remark	Allows explanatory remarks to be inserted in a program.	To add a remark to the end of a line, precede remark with a single quotation mark (').

displays the numbers like this:

```
25.3          -16.7896     3          .45
```

A semicolon (;) tells the computer to put the output of the *next* PRINT statement on the same line. Thus,

```
10 PRINT 25.3, -16.7896;
20 PRINT 3, .45
```

produces this display:

```
25.3          -16.7896  3  .45
```

Notice what else the semicolon does: it turns off the zoning. The computer separated 3 from −16.7896 by just two spaces. This tells you that if you want to *control* the format of the display, separate the data with semicolons instead of commas.

PRINT alone (nothing after it) produces a blank line.

The variation PRINT USING lets you tell the computer how to display information. For example, PRINT USING can display part of a string or place dollar signs ($) or asterisks (*) along with numbers.

To see the formatting power of PRINT USING versus PRINT, let us look at an example. Suppose that you write a program that prints the amount of sales or value added tax a customer owes on a purchase. The tax rate is in the variable TAXRATE; the purchase price is in the variable PRICE. To print the tax, you use

```
20 TAX = PRICE*TAXRATE
30 PRINT "$";TAX
```

Now, if TAXRATE = .06 (for 6 percent) and PRICE = 19.95, the program gives the result

```
$ 1.197
```

Note that PRINT produces two undesirable features: it puts a space between $ and 1.197 and it gives three digits to the right of the decimal point rather than two. We could write the same program with PRINT USING as follows:

```
20 TAX = PRICE*TAXRATE
30 PRINT USING "$$##.##";TAX
```

where $$ tells the computer to precede TAX with $ and ##.## tells it to print TAX with no more than two digits to the right and left of the decimal. If we run this new program, the result is

```
$1.20
```

LPRINT and LPRINT USING are like PRINT and PRINT USING, but they send their output to the printer.

Data Definition Statements. The LET statement assigns the value of an *expression* to a variable. An expression is a combination of variables, numbers, and operations. It may be a single number (15), a simple combination (SALES–COSTS), or a complex formula (VAR+(GRADE(I)–GMEAN)^2).

If the expression is numeric, the variable will also be numeric, as in these examples:

```
10 LET PI = 3.141593
20 LET TAX = PRICE * .06
```

Similarly, if the expression is a string, the variable will be a string, as in

```
40 LET MESSAGE1$ = "Wrong answer."
```

(Remember, string variable names must end with a $.)

The word LET is optional, so these forms are just as good:

```
10 PI = 3.141593
20 TAX = PRICE * .06
40 MESSAGE1$ = "Wrong answer."
```

To assign values to many variables at once, you can put the values in a *DATA statement* and let the computer assign them with a *READ statement*. If, for example, we have an employee named Joe Jones, age 46, in the position of senior auditor, assigned employee number 1453, the DATA statement is

```
50 DATA "Joe Jones",46,"Sr. Auditor",1453
```

The READ statement

```
30 READ NAME$,AGE,POSITION$
```

assigns NAME$=Joe Jones, AGE=46, and POSITION$=Sr. Auditor.

READ statements read values from the next DATA statement in the program or continue where a previous READ left off. For example, the preceding READ statement at line 30 reads all but the final value in the DATA statement at line 50. Thus, if line 40 has the READ statement

```
40 READ EMP.NO
```

the variable EMP.NO will be assigned the value 1453.

The RESTORE statement lets you reread DATA statements. This is useful when reinitializing values for another run. For example, after a chess game ends, you would want to move all the pieces back to their initial positions for the next game.

Repetition Statement. The FOR-NEXT statement tells the computer to repeat a section of a program a specific number of times. The FOR part marks the beginning of the section and tells the computer how to count the repetitions. The NEXT part (farther along in the program) marks the end of the section.

A typical example of FOR-NEXT is

```
100 FOR J = 1 TO 5
 ..
 ..
 ..
200 NEXT J
```

Here, J is the *loop variable*. The computer repeats everything between line 100 and line 200 for J = 1, 2, 3, 4, and 5. Whenever the computer reaches line 200, it adds 1 to J and begins another repetition if J is still not larger than 5.

For example, the following sequence calculates the average of five grades:

```
10 SUM = 0
20 FOR J = 1 TO 5
30 READ GRADE
40 SUM = SUM + GRADE
50 NEXT J
60 AVER = SUM/5
70 PRINT "Average =";AVER
80 DATA 65, 70, 80, 83, 57
90 END
```

Here, the computer repeats lines 30 and 40 five times, adding a different grade into SUM each time.

Occasionally we want to add something other than 1 to the loop variable each time. This requires us to put the word STEP and the step size at the end of the FOR statement. For example, the following program draws a diagonal line on the screen:

```
10 FOR J = 10 TO 1 STEP -1
20 PRINT TAB(J),"/"
30 NEXT J
40 END
```

Here, the computer adds −1 to J each time it reaches line 30.

Unconditional Transfer Statement. GOTO makes the computer leave where it is and continue at a specified line. You can use a GOTO statement to skip over or repeat part of a program. For example, in the following short program, the GOTO in line 70 sends the computer back to read the next set of data. It continues determining new inventory levels until it simply runs out of data.

```
10 DATA 100,10,250,25,200,30,400,50
20 READ OLDINV,SALES
30 LET NEWINV = OLDINV-SALES
40 PRINT "Old Inventory Level =";OLDINV
50 PRINT "Sales =";SALES
60 PRINT "New Inventory Level =";NEWINV
70 GOTO 20
```

Decision-Making Statements. The usual way to force a computer to make a decision is through an IF-THEN statement. This statement works as follows:

1. If the condition after IF is true, the computer does whatever follows THEN.
2. If the condition after IF is false, the computer proceeds to the next statement.

Typical examples of IF-THEN statements are:

```
IF BALANCE < 0 THEN PRINT "You are overdrawn"
IF COLUMN > 80 THEN PRINT "Point off screen"
IF GUESS = ANSWER THEN GOTO 1000
```

The condition after IF must be something that is either true or false. It cannot just be a number, variable, or string. Table 3-6 lists the operators you can use in the condition; note especially the odd forms for "not equal to," "less than or equal to," and "greater than or equal to."

The logical operators AND, OR, and XOR allow you to combine conditions with the usual logical meanings; AND means both, OR means either or both, and XOR means either but not both. For example, to check whether COLUMN is on the screen, we use the statement

```
IF COLUMN < 1 OR COLUMN > 80 THEN PRINT "Point off screen"
```

TABLE 3-6. OPERATORS USED IN IF-THEN STATEMENTS

Operator	*True If*	*Examples*
=	Equal to	IF GUESS = ANSWER THEN GOTO 1000
<>	Not equal to	IF GUESS<>ANSWER THEN PRINT "Wrong"
<	Less than	IF BAL < 0 THEN PRINT "Overdrawn"
>	Greater than	IF GUESS > ANSWER THEN PRINT "High"
<=	Less than or equal to	IF SPEED <= SAFE THEN PRINT "Safe"
>=	Greater than or equal to	IF TEMP >= BOIL.POINT THEN PRINT "Boiling"
AND	Both expressions true	IF GUESS1 = ANSWER1 AND GUESS2 = ANSWER2 THEN PRINT "Both correct!"
OR	Either or both expressions true	IF COLUMN > 80 OR LINE > 25 THEN PRINT "Point off screen"
XOR	Either expression true, but not both	IF GUESS1 = ANSWER1 XOR GUESS2 = ANSWER2 THEN PRINT "One is wrong"

Similarly, to determine if TEMP is in the comfort range, we use the statement

```
IF TEMP > LOW AND TEMP < HIGH THEN PRINT "In comfort range"
```

Although we have shown simple examples in which PRINT follows THEN, we could use any BASIC statement or sequence of statements on one line (separated by colons).

We may also tell the computer to follow another path if the condition is false. This involves placing ELSE after THEN. For example, to keep track of your checking account, you could use the statement

```
IF BALANCE < 0 THEN PRINT "You are overdrawn!"
  ELSE PRINT BALANCE
```

You can also put IF statements *inside* IF statements. For instance, the checking account program could warn you when your balance goes below $5.00, as follows:

```
IF BALANCE < 0 THEN PRINT "You are overdrawn!"
  ELSE IF BALANCE < 5 THEN PRINT "You are
  below $5" ELSE PRINT BALANCE
```

For example, a computer-aided instruction program might ask a student whether he or she wants addition, subtraction, multiplication, or division problems. It would then transfer control to the appropriate part of the program based on the answer. We could implement this as follows:

```
10 PRINT "What type of problems do you want?"
20 PRINT "Enter 1 for addition, 2 for subtraction,"
30 PRINT "3 for multiplication, or 4 for division"
40 INPUT TYPE
50 IF TYPE < 1 OR TYPE > 4 THEN GOTO 70
60 ON TYPE GOTO 1000, 2000, 3000, 4000
70 PRINT "You may only enter 1, 2, 3, or 4."
80 PRINT "Please try again."
90 GOTO 10
```

Line 40 uses INPUT, a statement we have not yet described. The INPUT statement simply accepts whatever the operator types and assigns it a name (TYPE, in this case).

Line 60 makes the computer go to line 1000 if TYPE is 1, to line 2000 if TYPE is 2, to line 3000 if TYPE is 3, or to line 4000 if TYPE is 4.

Line 50 prevents TYPE from falling outside its limits. If we did not have line 50, the computer would continue to the next line if the student entered 0 or a number between 5 and 255; it would print an error message if the student entered a number that was negative or greater than 256.

ON-GOTO has many uses. For example, an arithmetic quiz program could use it to choose among such messages as "Too high," "Too low," or "You are right! Do you want to try another problem?" It could also be used to calculate income tax, where the rate depends on the tax bracket. In short, ON-GOTO is handy in any application where the program must choose from among several paths.

Subroutine Statements. GOSUB is like GOTO except that GOSUB transfers control to a *subroutine* rather than to another part of the main program. A subroutine is a group of instructions that performs a particular task at several places in the main program.

For example, we could apply GOSUB in the computer-aided instruction program we just used to illustrate ON-GOTO. If a student enters an incorrect answer, a message might say

```
That is the wrong answer.
Do you want to try again?
Please enter Y for yes or N for no.
```

Of course, you *could* have identical PRINT statements that produce this message in all four sections, but that would be needlessly repetitive. A better approach would be to put those PRINT statements in a subroutine, so they can be executed from any section. Figure 3-1 shows how this program might look.

After the computer executes the subroutine, it goes back to the line in the program that follows GOSUB. The statement that tells the computer to do this is RETURN. Every subroutine must end with a RETURN.

In Figure 3-1, the RETURN at line 5040 makes the computer resume at line 1060, 2080, 3070, or 4100, depending on whether GOSUB 5000 occurred in the addition, subtraction, multiplication, or division section.

As does ON-GOTO, the ON-GOSUB statement makes the computer select one of several possible destinations. However, ON-GOSUB's destinations are subroutines rather than lines in the main program. For example, if the addition, subtraction, multiplication, and division

```
10 PRINT "What type of problems do you want?"
20 PRINT "Enter 1 for addition, 2 for subtraction,"
30 PRINT "3 for multiplication, or 4 for division."
40 INPUT TYPE
50 IF TYPE < 1 OR TYPE > 4 THEN GOTO 70
60 ON TYPE GOTO 1000, 2000, 3000, 4000
70 PRINT "You may only enter 1, 2, 3, or 4."
80 PRINT "Please try again."
90 GOTO 10
 ..
 ..
1000 (Addition statements start here)
 ..
 ..
1050 GOSUB 5000
1060 (After subroutine, computer returns here)
 ..
 ..
2000 (Subtraction statements start here)
 ..
 ..
2070 GOSUB 5000
2080 (After subroutine, computer returns here)
 ..
 ..
3000 (Multiplication statements start here)
 ..
 ..
3060 GOSUB 5000
3070 (After subroutine, computer returns here)
 ..
 ..
4000 (Division statements start here)
 ..
 ..
4090 GOSUB 5000
4100 (After subroutine, computer returns here)
 ..
 ..
5000 PRINT "That is the wrong answer."
5010 PRINT "Do you want to try again?"
5020 PRINT "Please enter Y for yes or N for no."
5030 INPUT RESPONSE$
5040 RETURN
```

Figure 3-1. Calling a Subroutine from a Program

portions of our computer-aided instruction program were subroutines, we could replace line 60 with the following:

```
60 ON TYPE GOSUB 1000, 2000, 3000, 4000
65 GOTO 10
```

Keyboard Input Statement. INPUT reads variable values from the keyboard and allows an optional message that tells the operator what to enter. BASIC will add a question mark to the end of the message automatically. If you omit the message, the computer will simply display a question mark as the prompt.

INPUT is normally used to obtain one variable at a time. For example,

```
20 INPUT "What is your name";NAME$
```

reads a name from the keyboard and puts it in NAME$. When the computer executes this statement, the screen shows

```
What is your name?  Pat Johnson
```

where **Pat Johnson** is the user's response. Thereafter, you can display Pat's name with **PRINT NAME$**.

INPUT also lets you display messages without a question mark. Simply put a comma, rather than a semicolon, after the prompt string. For example,

```
40 INPUT "Enter your age:",AGE
```

displays *Enter your age:* (no question mark) and calls the user's response AGE.

Although our examples showed INPUTs that required just one response from the user, you can call for several items at one time. For example,

```
50 INPUT "Enter your name and age, separated by a comma:",
   NAME$,AGE
```

reads a name and calls it NAME$, then reads a number and calls it AGE. INPUT variables may be strings or numbers, in any combination.

Data File Statements. Data files are the computerized equivalent of an office filing system. The disk is like a file cabinet, and the data files on it are like electronic file folders. Just as with a file folder, you must first open a data file, then add new information to it or remove old information from it, and finally close it.

OPEN is, reasonably enough, the BASIC statement that opens a data file. An OPEN statement must include the file's name (and, if it is on a drive other than the active drive, the drive name, A: or B:) and what you plan to do with the file.

Your plans may include creating a new file (specify **FOR OUTPUT**), reading data from a file (specify **FOR INPUT**), or adding data to a file (specify **FOR APPEND**). You must also give the data file a number (1, 2, or 3), which you can later use as shorthand for the file's name and drive. Note that you can have only three open files at a time.

Typical OPEN statements thus look like

1. OPEN "GRADES" FOR OUTPUT AS 1
   This creates the new file GRADES on the currently active disk drive and assigns it file number 1.
2. OPEN "B:OVERDUE" FOR INPUT AS 2
   This allows the user to read data from the file OVERDUE on drive B and assigns it file number 2.
3. OPEN "ABSENT" FOR APPEND AS 3
   This allows the user to add new data to the file ABSENT on the currently active disk drive and assigns it file number 3.

The primary statement that adds data to a file is PRINT#. A typical example is

```
100 PRINT#1, "John Smith", 35
```

This adds the string John Smith and the number 35 to the end of file number 1. Of course, a previous statement must have OPENed that file or the computer will report an error.

The primary statement that reads data from a file is INPUT#. A typical example is

```
200 INPUT#2, ACCTNAME$, DAYSOVER, BALANCE
```

Not only must a previous statement have OPENed file number 2 FOR INPUT, but we must also know how file 2's contents are organized.

As you might expect, CLOSE is the BASIC statement that closes a file after you are finished with it. We can close file 2 with the statement

```
CLOSE 2
```

or we can close all opened files at once with

```
CLOSE
```

Screen Control Statements. CLS erases the screen and moves the cursor to the upper left-hand corner.

LOCATE moves the cursor to a specified row and column position on the screen, usually in preparation for a PRINT statement. Generally, LOCATE takes the form

```
LOCATE row,col
```

where *row* is a line number (1 to 25) and *col* is a column number (1 to 80). For example,

```
100 LOCATE 1,1
```

moves the cursor to the upper left-hand corner and

```
200 LOCATE ,1
```

moves the cursor to the leftmost column on the current line.

Program-Terminating Statements. END and STOP make the computer return control to the user. END automatically closes any OPEN data files whereas STOP does not.

END is a sensible way of terminating programs, although the PC does not require it. STOP lets the computer stop a program at any point. For example, we might activate a STOP if a student does not answer a question within 2 or 3 minutes. This would prevent the computer from waiting endlessly for an answer the student simply cannot provide.

Miscellaneous Statements. MOTOR controls a cassette recorder's motor, turning it off if it is on or on if it is off. The motor must be on before you can store anything on a cassette.

The REM (remark) statement serves only to explain the program to its users. The computer ignores REMs, but it includes them in listings.

For example, in the sequence

```
40 REM Print sales tax @ 6%, then the total
50 TAX = PRICE * .06
60 TOTAL = PRICE + TAX
70 PRINT "Sales Tax= "; TAX;" Total= "; TOTAL
```

the REM on line 40 tells the reader what lines 50, 60, and 70 do.

You can also place a remark on the same line as a statement, by preceding it with an apostrophe. Using this form, the preceding example becomes

```
50 TAX = PRICE * .06 ' Calculate sales tax @ 6%
60 TOTAL = PRICE + TAX ' Calculate total
70 PRINT "Sales Tax= "; TAX;" Total= "; TOTAL
```

Advanced Statements

Table 3-7 summarizes BASIC statements that are not used as often as the statements in Table 3-5. We will discuss only the random disk file statements, since the other statements are largely self-explanatory.

Random Disk Files. The data files we discussed earlier are well suited to holding data that you store or read all at once. However, to read a particular item, the computer must pass through all preceding items. This can be quite slow if the file is large.

Cassettes allow only this *sequential* kind of file, because tape is a sequential medium. But disks allow so-called *random* files, where the computer can reach any *record* (a fundamental group of items, such as the data for a particular student, employee, or patient) in about the same amount of time. A random file acts like a book; that is, you can flip to any page (access any record) without passing through all previous pages.

When would you use random files? Whenever you need to read or change individual records. With random files, for example, an accountant can change a single entry in a ledger and a teacher can correct or revise one student's test score.

Random files are convenient once you learn how to use them. It takes three operations to transfer data to or from a random file. You must first set up an area in memory (*a buffer*) to hold the data. To write data into a random file, you must store the data in the buffer and then transfer its contents to the disk file. To read data from a random file, you must read the disk data into the buffer and then access the data in your program.

Random files also differ from sequential files in the kind of data they can hold. Random files can hold only string data. Thus, if you want to store numbers in a random file, you must convert them to strings first. You will also have to convert them back to numbers when you use the file later.

As with a sequential file, you must *open* a random file before you can work with it. The only difference in the OPEN statement is that you

TABLE 3-7. ADVANCED STATEMENTS*

Statement	*Action*	*Comments*
	Date and Time Statements	
DATE$ = newdate$	Changes current date to newdate$.	The string newdate$ may take four forms: mm-dd-yy, mm/dd/yy, mm-dd-yyyy, mm/dd/yyyy
TIME$ = newtime$	Changes current time to newtime$.	The string newtime$ may take three forms: hh, hh:mm, hh:mm:ss
	Define Statement	
DEF FNname[(arg[,...])]=definition	Defines a function that you write.	
	Random Disk File Statements	
FIELD filenum,width AS x$[,width AS y$...]	Reserves space for string variables in a buffer.	
GET filenum[,recordnum]	Reads a record from a disk file into a buffer.	Opposite of PUT.
LSET fieldvar$ = progvar$ RSET fieldvar$ = progvar$	Stores the value of progvar$ into a buffer, left-justified (LSET) or right-justified (RSET).	LSET and RSET are used to prepare for a PUT statement.
OPEN [drivename:]filename AS filenum [LEN=reclen]	Allows a random file to accessed.	To close a random file, use the standard CLOSE statement.
PUT filenum[,recordnum]	Writes a record from a buffer to a disk file.	Opposite of GET.
	Key-Sensing Statements	
KEY(n) ON	Enables BASIC to check for function and cursor keys.	Must precede the first ON KEY statement. Advanced BASIC only.
KEY(n) OFF	Makes BASIC ignore key depressions.	Advanced BASIC only.

* Brackets indicate that the item(s) inside them are optional.

TABLE 3-7. (continued)

Statement	*Action*	*Comments*
KEY(n) STOP	Same as KEY OFF, but BASIC remembers a key depression, and will call subroutine as soon as KEY ON is executed.	Advanced BASIC only.
ON KEY(n) GOSUB line	Calls subroutine if key n is pressed.	Advanced BASIC only.
	Light Pen-Sensing Statements	
PEN ON	Enables BASIC to check for light pen operations.	Must precede the first PEN function or ON PEN statement.
PEN OFF	Makes BASIC ignore light pen operations.	
PEN STOP	Same as PEN OFF, but BASIC remembers light pen operations, and will call subroutine as soon as PEN ON is executed.	Advanced BASIC only.
ON PEN GOSUB line	Calls subroutine if light pen is ON.	Advanced BASIC only.
	Joystick-Sensing Statements	
STRIG(button) ON	Enables BASIC to check for joystick buttons.	Must precede the first STRIG function or ON STRIG statement.
STRIG(button) OFF	Makes BASIC ignore joystick operations.	
STRIG(button) STOP	Same as STRIG OFF, but BASIC remembers joystick buttons and will call subroutine as soon as STRIG ON is executed.	Advanced BASIC only.
ON STRIG(button) GOSUB line	Calls subroutine if button is pressed.	Advanced BASIC only.

may end it with *LEN* = *reclen*, where *reclen* is the number of bytes (characters) in a record. Records may be from 1 to 32,767 bytes long; the default (if you do not specify otherwise) is 128 bytes. This tells the computer the size of the basic unit of information in your files.

For example, suppose that you want to store the names and telephone numbers of your friends in a random file. Each record in that file would contain the name and telephone number of one person. If you allow 20 characters for a name and 12 characters for a number, you might use the following statement to create the file on drive B:

```
10 OPEN "B:PHONE" AS 1 LEN=32
```

What would happen if you omitted LEN? If you had used

```
10 OPEN "B:PHONE" AS 1
```

the computer would (by default) make each record 128 bytes long instead of 32. Since you only need 32 bytes, the extra 96 bytes in each record would go unused. That means if you put the names and numbers of 100 friends in the PHONE file (being a popular person), you waste 9600 bytes. Obviously, that would be an inefficient use of disk space.

As we just mentioned, all data you transfer to or from a random file must pass through a buffer. You set up the buffer with a FIELD statement, which has the general form

```
FIELD filenum,width AS x$[,width AS y$...]
```

where x$ is the name you assign to a string in the record and *width* is the number of characters in x$.

For example, the statement

```
30 FIELD 1, 20 AS NAME$, 12 AS TNUMBER$
```

sets up a 32-character buffer for file 1 (PHONE in the preceding OPEN statement) and reserves the first 20 positions for the string variable NAME$ and the remaining 12 positions for the string variable TNUMBER$. FIELD does the same thing for random files that DIM does for arrays: it just reserves space in memory.

Before you can store data onto a disk, you must put the data in the buffer with an LSET or RSET statement. LSET and RSET have the following general forms,

```
LSET fieldvar$ = progvar$
RSET fieldvar$ = progvar$
```

where *fieldvar$* is a string variable in the FIELD statement and *progvar$* is a string variable in your program.

LSET and RSET differ in that LSET stores the string left-justified whereas RSET stores it right-justified. The computer fills any unused positions in the buffer with spaces. For example, the statements

```
100 NAME1$ = "Johnny Hodges"
110 RSET NAME$ = NAME1$
```

puts the 13-character string *Johnny Hodges* in the NAME$ portion of the buffer. And since NAME$ is 20 characters wide, the string is preceded with seven spaces. It looks like

```
bbbbbbbJohnny Hodges
```

where the b's are spaces. Similarly, you can put Mr. Hodges's telephone number in the buffer with

```
120 PHONE1$ = "307-555-2121"
130 RSET TNUMBER$ = PHONE1$
```

Now that both records are in the buffer, you can write them to the disk using the PUT statement. PUT has the general form

```
PUT filenum[,recordnum]
```

where the optional *recordnum* is the number of the record in the buffer. Therefore, to write the NAME$ and TNUMBER$ strings to file 1 (PHONE), as the first record in that file, you might use

```
150 PUT 1,1
```

If you omit *recordnum*, it is assumed to be the next available record. (In the example, a subsequent PUT 1 statement would write the buffer to disk as record *2*.)

A typical sequence of statements for writing data to a random file on disk is

```
10 OPEN "B:PHONE" AS 1 LEN=32 ' Open PHONE file
20 FIELD 1, 20 AS NAME$, 12 AS TNUMBER$ ' Set up buffer
30 NAME1$ = "Johnny Hodges" ' Define first field
40 RSET NAME$ = NAME1$ ' Put this field in buffer
50 PHONE1$ = "307-555-2121" ' Define second field
60 RSET TNUMBER$ = PHONE1$ ' Put this field in buffer
70 PUT 1,1 ' Write the record to disk
80 CLOSE 1 ' Close the PHONE file
```

Note the final CLOSE.

Reading a file is similar. To begin, you must OPEN the file and set up the buffer with FIELD. The GET statement reads a record from disk. GET's general form is

```
GET filenum[,recordnum]
```

For example, if you insert in the preceding example

```
75 GET 1,1
```

the computer reads NAME$, and then TNUMBER$, into the buffer.

That's all there is to a read operation! Once the strings are in the buffer, your programs can use them like any other string variables. For instance, you could display NAME$ and TNUMBER$ with

```
90 PRINT NAME$, TNUMBER$
```

With these additional read statements, the complete program is

```
10 OPEN "B:PHONE" AS 1 LEN=32 ' Open PHONE file
20 FIELD 1, 20 AS NAME$, 12 AS TNUMBER$ ' Set up buffer
30 NAME1$ = "Johnny Hodges" ' Define first field
40 RSET NAME$ = NAME1$ ' Put this field in buffer
50 PHONE1$ = "307-555-2121" ' Define second field
60 RSET TNUMBER$ = PHONE1$ ' Put this field in buffer
70 PUT 1,1 ' Write the record to disk
75 GET 1,1 ' Read the record from disk
80 CLOSE 1 ' Close the PHONE file
90 PRINT NAME$, TNUMBER$ ' Display the record
```

For more information on random files, see Appendix B of IBM's BASIC manual.

3.4 FUNCTIONS

BASIC has built-in programs called *functions*. For example, the function SQR calculates a square root and SIN finds the sine of an angle. Table 3-8 summarizes the BASIC functions in four groups: numerical, string, keyboard input, and date and time.

Numerical Functions

Numerical functions produce numerical results. The operand can be either a number or an expression. For example, SQR(2) takes the square root of 2, and SQR(3*V) takes the square root of three times *V*, where *V*

TABLE 3-8. COMMON FUNCTIONS*

Function	*Result*	*Comments*
	Numerical Functions	
ABS(x)	Absolute value.	Magnitude of a number, ignoring its sign. Always positive or zero.
ATN(x)	Arctangent.	Angle is in radians.
CINT(x)	Whole number closest to *x*. See also FIX(x) and INT(x).	If *x* is not between −32,768 and 32,767, the computer generates an *Overflow* error.
COS(x)	Cosine.	Angle is in radians.
EXP(x)	Raises e to the *x* power.	*e* = 2.718282
FIX(x)	Whole number part of *x*. See also CINT(x) and INT(x).	See CINT comment.
INT(x)	Largest whole number less than or equal to *x*.	
LOG(x)	Natural logarithm of *x*.	Natural logarithm is logarithm to the base *e*.
RND	Random number.	
SGN(x)	Sign of *x*.	SGN returns 1 if *x* is positive, 0 if *x* is zero, or −1 if *x* is negative.
SIN(x)	Sine.	Angle is in radians.
SQR(x)	Square root.	If *x* is negative, the computer generates an *Illegal function call* error.
TAN(x)	Tangent.	Angle is in radians.
	String Functions	
INSTR([n,]x$,y$)	Position of first occurrence of y$ in x$, starting at position n.	If *n* is greater than the length of x$, INSTR returns 0.
LEFT$(x$,n)	Leftmost *n* characters of x$.	If *n* is greater than the length of x$, LEFT$ returns the entire string.
LEN(x$)	Number of characters in x$.	Unprintable characters and blanks are counted.
MID$(x$,n[,m])	The *m* characters that start at position n.	If m is omitted, MID$ returns all remaining characters in x$.
RIGHT$(x$,n)	Rightmost *n* characters of x$.	If *n* is greater than the length of x$, RIGHT$ returns the entire string.
SPACE$(n)	Inserts *n* spaces. See also SPC(n).	Value n can range from 0 to 255.
SPC(n)	Prints *n* spaces. See also SPACE$(n).	May only be used in a PRINT, LPRINT, or PRINT# statement.

* Brackets indicate that the item(s) inside them are optional.

TABLE 3-8. (continued)

Function	*Result*	*Comments*
STR$(x)	String representation of numerical value *x*.	Opposite of VAL(x$).
STRING$(n,x$)	String of length *n* composed entirely of the first character of x$.	
TAB(n)	Tabs to position *n*.	May only be used in a PRINT, LPRINT, or PRINT# statement.
VAL(x$)	Numerical value of x$.	Opposite of STR$(x).
	Keyboard Input Functions	
INKEY$	Reads a character from the keyboard.	If no key is available, INKEY$ returns the null (empty) string.
INPUT$(n)	Reads n characters from the keyboard.	Characters are not displayed.
	Date and Time Functions	
DATE$	The current date, in the form *mm-dd-yyyy*.	
TIME$	The current time, in the form *hh:mm:ss*.	

is a variable. Most of these functions are self-explanatory, so we will discuss only a few special features or peculiarities.

The trigonometric functions ATN, COS, SIN, and TAN all require an argument in *radians*. If your angle is in degrees, you must first multiply it by $\pi/180$ (where $\pi = 3.141593$) to convert it to radians. For example, to print the sine of 15.5°, enter

```
10 PI = 3.141593
20 PRINT SIN(15.5*PI/180)
```

INT gives the integer (whole number) part of a number. That is, INT(37.3) = 37 and INT(−37.5) = −38. Thus, INT finds the largest whole number that is smaller than its argument.

RND produces a sequence of numbers between 0 and 1 with no apparent pattern. That is, RND makes the computer pick a number at random, just as if it had thrown a pair of dice or spun a roulette wheel. This is not only useful in computer games, but also provides needed variety in instructional and statistical programs.

To make the computer choose a random *whole* number between LOW and HIGH, we must use a multiplying factor and the INT function.

That is,

```
D = INT(RND*(HIGH+1-LOW))+LOW
```

will do the job. Thus, for example,

1. D = INT(RND*6)+1 chooses a random whole number between 1 and 6 (equivalent to the roll of an honest die).
2. COL = INT(RND*80)+1 chooses a random column on the computer screen.

Although RND *appears* to produce numbers that are truly random, it does not. Instead, RND produces numbers in a specific sequence. It operates like a phony mind reader whose assistant always picks the third card from the top, then the fourth card from the bottom, and so on.

Although RND always chooses numbers from a given sequence, you can make it choose from a *different* sequence each time. You do this by preceding RND with a RANDOMIZE statement. RANDOMIZE takes the general form

```
RANDOMIZE(n)
```

where *n* can be any whole number between −32768 and 32767. Thus, *n* selects one of more than 65,000 different sequences for RND to choose numbers from.

For example,

```
10 RANDOMIZE(100)
20 COL = INT(RND*80)+1
```

chooses columns on the screen in one sequence, while

```
10 RANDOMIZE(200)
20 COL = INT(RND*80)+1
```

chooses columns in an entirely different sequence. If you want to start RND at a different point every time, you could ask the operator for an essentially random input, such as the second count on his or her wristwatch. Your program could then use the input in RANDOMIZE.

String Functions

String functions operate on messages, labels, and other text material. For example, the following sequence uses RIGHT$ to display the last five characters (the U.S. ZIP Code) of the string ADDRESS$:

```
10 ADDRESS$ = "Pittsburgh, PA 15214"
20 PRINT RIGHT$(ADDRESS$,5)
RUN
15214
Ok
```

The functions LEFT$, MID$, and RIGHT$ let you use parts of a string at different points in a program. You can thereby pick out a person's first or last name, the local or area part of a telephone number, or a street number. For example, if the string NAME$ holds the characters *Mr. John C. Smith*, we could create a personalized advertising letter as follows:

```
10 TITL$=LEFT$(NAME$,4)
20 FNAME$=MID$(NAME$,5,4)
30 LNAME$=RIGHT$(NAME$,5)
40 PRINT "Dear ";TITL$;LNAME$;":"
50 PRINT
60 PRINT TAB(5);"Would you like the name ";FNAME$;" ";
   LNAME$;" to be associated with success?"
70 PRINT TAB(5);"Yes, ";TITL$;" ";LNAME$;", YOU can";
   "be a dynamic, successful person if you attend";
   "our seminar!"
```

Obviously, as you have probably noted in your daily mail, this approach allows advertisers to sprinkle your name, address, city, and state throughout their letters—just as if they actually knew you as something more than TITL$,FNAME$,LNAME$.

The LEN$ function determines the number of characters (including spaces) in a string. You can use LEN$ to center titles. Another handy function for formatting is SPACE$, which inserts a selected number of spaces. SPC and TAB also let you format material on the screen or printer.

Finally, the STR$ and VAL$ functions convert a number to a string or a string to a number, respectively. These functions are useful for processing data in a report.

If, for example, your report includes sales figures by department, you might want to print a total. However, you cannot simply add the numbers as they are, since they are in text form. You can use VAL$ to convert the numbers into ordinary numerical form, add them, and then use STR$ to convert the total back to text form. This awkward difference between text and numbers is one reason why we have recently begun to see programs like Lotus 1-2-3 and Context MBA that can process both text and data.

The final string function, STRING$, builds a new string from a single character. STRING$ is useful for formatting a printed page. For example, the following statements print asterisks across all 80 columns of a page:

```
10 A$ = "*"
20 LPRINT STRING$(80,A$)
```

Keyboard Input Functions

INKEY$ and INPUT$ allow the computer to accept commands from the keyboard. INPUT$ waits for a specified number of characters, whereas INKEY$ reads in a single character or the empty (null) string if no character is immediately available.

You generally use INPUT$ to accept a known number of keystrokes. For example, the following sequence waits for the operator to enter his or her age as a two-digit number:

```
10 PRINT "Please enter your age"
20 AGE$ = INPUT$(2)
```

INKEY$ is convenient for determining whether the operator is currently pressing a key. For example, suppose that you have a program that the operator can stop at any time to examine the screen information. To let the operator restart the program, you might include the sequence

```
100 PRINT "Press any key to continue"
110 START$ = INKEY$
120 IF START$ = " " THEN GOTO 110
```

```
 10 PRINT "Press any key to get a new problem."
 20 START$ = INPUT$(1) ' Wait for a key
 30 GOSUB 1000 ' Display the problem
 40 PRINT "Enter your answer as three digits."
 50 TIME$ = "0" ' Start time at zero
 60 MINUTE$ = MID$(TIME$,5,1) ' Read minutes value
 70 IF VAL(MINUTES$) > 0 THEN GOTO 130
 80 FIRSTKEY$ = INKEY$ ' Is student pressing a key?
 90 IF FIRSTKEY$ = " " THEN GOTO 60 ' If not, keep waiting
100 TWOKEY$ = INPUT$(2) ' If so, read remaining keys
110 ANSWER$ = FIRSTKEY$ + TWOKEYS$ ' Combine the keystrokes
120 GOTO 2000 ' Check the student's answer
130 PRINT "Sorry, your time is up."
140 PRINT "Do you want to know the correct answer?"
150 PRINT "Press Y for yes or N for no."
160 RESPONSE$ = INPUT$(1)
170 IF RESPONSE$ = "y" THEN GOTO 3000 ELSE GOTO 10
```

Figure 3-2. A Program That Uses TIME$

Date and Time Functions

DATE$ and TIME$ read the current settings of the computer's built-in calendar and clock. With TIME$, you can calculate how long a program takes to run, how long it takes you to run a mile, or just about anything else you care to measure. For example, Figure 3-2 shows a computer-aided instruction program that displays arithmetic problems to students. When the problem appears, the computer gives the student 1 minute to enter a three-digit answer. If he or she fails to respond in time, the PC asks if the student wants the correct answer. Note that here, line 50 uses the TIME$ *statement*, whereas line 60 uses the time *function*.

3.5 LEAVING BASIC

There are three ways to leave BASIC and return to DOS:

1. Flip the power switch off and then back on again.
2. Press the Ctrl, Alt, and Del keys simultaneously. Del is the decimal point key in the numeric keypad.
3. Type the command **SYSTEM** and then press Enter.

Chapter 4

DISK OPERATING SYSTEM

As we discussed in Chapter 1, a disk drive requires a disk operating system (DOS). This is a set of programs that helps you to use the disk. A DOS lets the user handle collections of information called *files*; the user can create new files, copy files, list the directory, delete files, and do other jobs.

Several companies sell disk operating systems for the PC, but we will discuss only the standard DOS sold by IBM. This DOS is called PC-DOS or IBM DOS.

We used 3 DOS programs in Chapter 2: FORMAT to prepare a disk, DISKCOPY to back up the DOS disk, and DIR (directory) to find out what files a disk contains. IBM DOS includes 10 other programs. You can run them just like FORMAT, DISKCOPY, or DIR by entering their names.

This chapter covers all 13 DOS commands. As usual, we divide them into two groups: common and advanced. To use DOS effectively, you must be familiar with DOS files, so we will start with that subject.

4.1 DOS FILES

A file is any collection of information; it may be a program, a document, inventory records, or a set of numbers. Every file has a unique *filename*.

As noted earlier, you must put the drive name (A or B) in front of the filename if the file is not on the active drive.

Filename Extensions

DOS also lets you add an *extension* to a filename. The extension usually identifies what type the file is. For example, you might have TXT for a text file, DAT for a data file, DOC for a document, or INV for an inventory file. The extension allows you to determine quickly what kind of file you have and thus what you can do with it.

The extension appears at the end of the filename, separated from it by a period. It may be up to three characters. Thus typical filenames with extensions are WILL.TXT, PAYRATES.DAT, and SHOP1.INV.

You can compare adding extensions to the practice of putting colored tabs, tags, or markers on file folders. A realtor could, for example, mark his or her files with different colors to indicate single-family houses, condominiums, commercial property, industrial property, offices, rentals, lots, and acreage. On the computer, he or she would give the different types of files different extensions: HSE for house, CDM for condominium, CML for commercial, IND for industrial, OFC for office, RNT for rental, LOT for lots, and ACR for acreage.

Why would you want an extension? There are many reasons, including the following:

1. You can tell immediately from the extension what the file contains. You will not accidentally try to execute a file that contains data, use a word processor on a file that does not contain text, or plot a file that does not contain numbers.
2. DOS and other programs often allow you to operate on all files of a certain type with a single command. You can, for example, list all text files, copy all data files to another disk, or delete all BASIC programs from a disk with one command. We will explain how to do this later in this chapter.
3. Some programs operate only on files of a particular type. Thus a text processor may require a file of type .TXT, BASIC may require a file of type .BAS, and a statistical analysis or plotting program may require a file of type .DAT.

   Programs may also identify their outputs with extensions. For example, the popular WordStar word processor not only saves a copy of a text file when so instructed but also saves the old version with the extension .BAK. The user can thus readily identify old versions for renaming, transfer to another disk, or deletion.

4. Extensions can allow you to group files to meet your particular needs. If, for example, you are a teacher with five class periods, you could use extensions P1 through P5 to separate the periods. You could then have files ROSTER, GRADES, ATTEND, and HOMEWK for each class. That is, the files for period 2 would be ROSTER.P2, GRADES.P2, ATTEND.P2, and HOMEWK.P2. You would be able, as we will show later, to work on all files with a particular name (e.g., all ROSTER files) or with a particular extension (e.g., all P2 files).

Since some extensions have special meanings, you should not use them for your own purposes. A typical example is .BAS, which BASIC uses as an extension for all program files. Extensions you should avoid (unless you are trying to create a file of that particular type) are

.ASM	.BAK	.BAS	.COM	.EXE
.LST	.MAP	.OBJ	.REF	.TMP

Operating on Groups of Files

As we just noted, one reason for choosing filenames and extensions carefully is that DOS allows you to operate on entire groups of similarly named files. You can thus, for example, copy or display a directory of a group of files with one typed command. The way to do this is by using "wild-card" characters; these special characters act as shorthand for "any character" or "any group of characters." You can compare them with the joker in popular card games, a free number in Bingo, or a blank tile in Scrabble.

The character ? means "any single character." You can put ? anywhere in a file name or extension—even several times. For example, the command

```
DIR GRADES.P?
```

displays a list of all files named GRADES.P, regardless of what character follows P. Similarly, if we had a set of annual sales reports under the names ANNSLS.Y79, ANNSLS.Y80, ANNSLS.Y81, and so on, the command

```
DIR ANNSLS.Y8?
```

would display a list of all annual sales report files for the 1980s. Note that ANNSLS.Y79 would not be listed. The alternatives would be a series of commands or a listing that would contain files that are not of current interest.

The * (asterisk) is an even more all-encompassing wild card. It tells DOS that any character can occupy that position and all remaining positions in the filename or extension. For example, the command,

```
DIR GRADES.*
```

would display all GRADES files, regardless of their extensions. On the other hand,

```
DIR *.P3
```

would display all P3 files, regardless of their filenames. You could even have

```
DIR PAY*.*
```

which would display all files that have PAY as the first three letters of their filenames.

The key point here is that you should name your files carefully and systematically. The idea is really the same as labeling file folders in a cabinet so that anyone can locate desired information; after all, you might want someone to find all contract files or all files for a particular case or customer. If you name your files carefully, the wild-card characters (? and *) will allow you to work with them in groups, rather than one at a time.

Choosing Filenames. Table 4-1 summarizes the formal rules for choosing filenames and extensions (i.e., filespecs), but you should

TABLE 4-1. SUMMARY OF FILESPEC RULES

Term	*Description*
d:	The drive name; either A: or B:. Only necessary if the file is not on the active drive.
filename	The name of a disk file. Filenames can be up to eight characters long. The legal characters are A-Z 0-9 $ & # @ ! % ' ( ) - { } _ ^ ~ `
.ext	An optional filename extension. Extensions can be one to three characters long. Legal characters are the same as for filenames.

remember the ordinary commonsense rules that apply to any kind of filing. These rules include the following:

1. Filenames should be no longer than eight characters. DOS will accept longer filenames, but it will list only the first eight characters when you run a directory with DIR.
2. The filename should suggest the contents of the file. For example, ROSTER and PROFITS are more meaningful than R and P.
3. If several files are to contain similar information, differentiate them by their extensions. For example, the names PROFITS.2Q and PROFITS.3Q effectively tell the user that he or she is working with profits from the second and third quarters.
4. The filename should be easy to type without errors. Whenever possible, avoid similar-looking characters, such as the letter O and the number 0, letter I and number 1, and letter S and number 5.

4.2 COMMON DOS COMMANDS

Table 4-2 summarizes the common DOS commands. FORMAT, DISK-COPY, and DIR act on the entire disk. COPY, ERASE, RENAME, and TYPE act on individual files or groups of files.

COPY Command

As you might expect, COPY copies files. If you copy them onto another disk, you can give them the same names as the originals. If you copy files onto the same disk, you must rename them. Either way, COPY does not affect the original files.

COPY obviously requires two filespecs, a source and a destination; the source comes first. You may omit the destination's name if it is the same as the source's. Typical examples of copying a single file are

COPY PAYROLL B:	(Copy PAYROLL to drive B.)
COPY CHECKS B:OLDCHECKS	(Copy CHECKS to drive B and rename it OLDCHECKS.)
COPY CONTRACT BIGCASE.CON	(Copy CONTRACT to same disk and rename it BIGCASE.CON.)
COPY WILL.GEN WILL.TXT	(Copy WILL.GEN to same disk and rename it WILL.TXT.)

TABLE 4-2. COMMON DOS COMMANDS

Command	Action	Comments
COPY old-filespec [new-filespec]	Copies files.	
DIR [filespec]	Displays name, size, and date of file(s) on a disk.	If you omit the filespec, DIR summarizes the entire disk.
DISKCOPY [source-drive] [target-drive]	Copies an entire disk.	Target disk need not be FORMATted.
ERASE filespec	Deletes a file.	
FORMAT [d:][/S]	Prepares a disk to accept DOS files. The optional /S puts a copy of DOS on the disk.	*Deletes any files currently on the disk.*
RENAME old-filespec new-filename[.ext]	Changes the name of a file.	
TYPE filespec	Displays the contents of a file on the screen.	

By using ? and * characters, you can copy a group of files with one COPY command, as in these examples:

COPY BIGCASE.* B:	(Copy all BIGCASE files to drive B.)
COPY BIGCASE.Y* B:	(Same, but copy only BIGCASE files whose extensions start with Y.)
COPY *.GEN B:*.TXT	(Copy all files with extensions of GEN to drive B; replace GEN with TXT.)

You can use COPY to make backup copies for records or insurance, initial versions, and extra copies for experimentation. Thus, for example, an attorney might start a contract for a particular client by copying a file with a standard form. Similarly, a teacher might want to revise a multiple-choice test while still retaining the old version. A nice feature of starting with COPY is that you can experiment with the copy as much as you want. You can always go back to the original version if the changes do not work out.

DIR (Directory) Command

DIR displays information about files on a disk. It tells you three things about each file: filename and extension, size in characters, and the date it was most recently saved.

For example, if you run DIR for the IBM DOS disk, the entry for the ART program is

```
ART      BAS      1920  08-04-81
```

This tells you that ART is a BASIC program file (its extension is BAS), is 1920 bytes long, and was put onto disk on August 4, 1981.

You can follow DIR with a filespec. This limits the display to files in a particular group. Typical examples are

DIR	(Display all files on the active drive.)
DIR B:	(Display all files on drive B.)
DIR B:*.BAS	(Display all BASIC program files on drive B.)
DIR B:NEW*.BAS	(Same, but display only BASIC programs whose filenames start with NEW.)

If your disk has many files, the display may move up the screen so fast that you cannot read it. To stop the scrolling temporarily, press Ctrl and Num Lock. Later you can press the space bar to start the display again. To stop the scrolling altogether, press Ctrl and Break simultaneously.

DISKCOPY Command

DISKCOPY copies an entire disk. The general form is:

```
DISKCOPY [source-drive] [target-drive]
```

Note that the source drive comes first. If the disk in the target drive has not been FORMATted, DOS will automatically format it before performing the DISKCOPY operation.

If you omit both drive designations, DISKCOPY performs a single-drive copy operation on the active drive. See Appendix A for a step-by-step DISKCOPY procedure.

ERASE Command

ERASE deletes files. It can delete a single file or an entire group of files. Typical examples are

ERASE PAYROLL.TXT	(Delete only PAYROLL.TXT.)
ERASE BIGCASE.*	(Delete every BIGCASE file.)
ERASE B:*.BAS	(Delete all BASIC program files on drive B.)
ERASE B:NEW*.BAS	(Delete only BASIC program files that begin with the word NEW.)

Be careful if you use ? and * to erase a group of files because a single misplaced character may result in the deletion of files you want to keep. To avoid disaster, run DIR with the filespec you plan to use with ERASE. DIR will provide a list of every file that ERASE will delete.

In theory, good programmers always erase files they no longer need. But in reality, most of us don't erase *anything* until the disk is full and we can't fit anything more on it. That is, we usually treat a disk like a file cabinet or desk drawer; we just keep tossing things in until it is absolutely full. Thus, we will not waste our time or yours providing guidelines that no one will ever follow.

FORMAT Command

FORMAT prepares a disk to accept DOS files. You can compare formatting a disk with drawing lines on a baseball or football field or marking the origins and axes on a piece of graph paper. That is, formatting prepares the disk for use, but it does not actually do anything with it.

You can follow FORMAT with a drive name to specify the disk to be formatted, as in

```
FORMAT B:
```

A further option is a final /S, which puts a copy of the main DOS programs on the disk, as in

```
FORMAT B:/S
```

The main DOS programs are COPY, DATE, DIR, ERASE, RENAME, TIME, and TYPE. If you want any additional DOS commands, you must COPY their programs from the DOS disk.

You use the /S option when you want to be able to operate directly from a disk after turning the power on. If a disk with DOS is in drive A when you turn on the power, the PC will start up DOS and show the DOS prompt, *A*〉. However, if you want to use a BASIC program on the disk, you still must insert the DOS disk to load BASIC.

RENAME Command

RENAME changes a file's name. This command obviously requires two filespecs; the old filespec comes first. For example, the command

```
RENAME B:PAYROLL.TXT OLDPAY
```

changes the name of PAYROLL.TXT on drive B to OLDPAY. The command

```
RENAME B:ROSTER *.P1
```

changes the name of ROSTER on drive B to ROSTER.P1, thus adding an extension to a filename that did not have one. You can also *change* a filename extension. For example,

```
RENAME DATES.Y83 *.Y84
```

changes DATES.Y83 on the active drive to DATES.Y84.

Finally, RENAME can preserve files while you are deleting an entire group. For instance, suppose that you have files named PROFITS.81, PROFITS.82, PROFITS.83, and PROFITS.84. If you want to delete all except PROFITS.83, you can do so with the sequence

```
RENAME PROFITS.83 TEMP
ERASE PROFITS.*
RENAME TEMP PROFITS.83
```

Here, TEMP serves as a temporary "hideout" for PROFITS.83, keeping it from being ERASEd.

TYPE Command

TYPE displays the contents of a file on the screen. You generally use it to just look at the information in a file, perhaps to check some detail (such as one employee's salary in a payroll file). However, TYPE does not work with BASIC program files; it shows nothing but "garbage" on the screen. To display a BASIC program, use BASIC's LIST command instead.

4.3 ADVANCED COMMANDS

Table 4-3 summarizes the less used DOS commands.

CHKDSK (Check Disk) Command

CHKDSK tells you how many files are on a disk and how many bytes (characters) are still available. It also reports on memory use. CHKDSK reports on the active drive unless you follow it with a drive name.

A typical report from CHKDSK looks like

```
160256 bytes total disk space
  8704 bytes in 2 hidden files
144384 bytes in 26 user files
  7168 bytes available on disk

 65536 bytes total memory
 53136 bytes free
```

Here, the "hidden files" (second line) are the primary DOS programs. They are hidden in that they are not listed by DIR.

The first four lines tell you the disk's status. This particular disk is nearly full, since only 7168 bytes of its 160,256-byte capacity are still available. Furthermore, because disks can hold 64 files, the third line tells you that this disk could accept 38 more files, provided that they do not occupy more than 7168 bytes.

The last two lines tell you that most of the memory is still available. That is helpful (you are unlikely to get an Insufficient Memory error), but if you enter a program or data file containing more than 7168 characters, you will have to save it on another disk.

As a rule of thumb, when you get down to about 5000 to 6000 free bytes on a disk, you should change disks. Disks are inexpensive, and you do not want to lose some work because a disk is full.

TABLE 4-3. ADVANCED DOS COMMANDS*

Command	*Action*	*Comments*
CHKDSK [d:]	Displays a disk and memory status report.	
COMP filespec [d:][filename[.ext]]	Compares two files.	See also DISKCOMP.
DATE	Lets you change the current date.	See also TIME.
DISKCOMP [d:] [d:]	Compares two disks.	See also COMP.
SYS d:	Copies operating system files from the active drive to the specified drive.	Target disk must be one formatted with FORMAT d: /S.
TIME	Lets you change the current time value.	See also DATE.

* Brackets indicate that the item(s) inside them are optional.

COMP (Compare) Command

COMP compares two disk files. You generally use COMP to verify a file after copying it. You can also use COMP if you suspect two files are identical and want to delete one. Perhaps, for example, you accidentally revised the same document twice and are not quite sure whether you changed it the same way both times.

COMP has the general form

```
COMP filespec [d:][filename[.ext]]
```

where the bracketed items are not entirely optional. COMP can take three forms:

```
COMP filespec d:                  (File has same name on different disks.)
COMP filespec filename[.ext]      (File has different names on same disk.)
COMP filespec d:filename[.ext]    (File has different names on different disks.)
```

Examples of these three forms are:

```
COMP ALIENS.BAS B:
COMP ALIENS.BAS ALNEW.BAS
COMP ALIENS.BAS B:ALNEW.BAS
```

To use COMP, put your disk(s) in the proper drive(s). When you press Enter, COMP displays the prompt

```
Mount diskette(s) with files to compare
and strike any key when ready
```

Since you have already done that, press the space bar. Now COMP begins comparing the files.

If the files match, the screen shows

```
Files compare ok
Compare more files (Y/N)?
```

If the files do not match, the screen shows something like

```
Compare error at offset D
File 1 = 74
File 2 = 44
```

where the *offset* tells where the mismatch occurred (in the assembly language programmer's *hexadecimal* notation, D here) and the two File values are the mismatched values (74 and 44 here).

Unless you are an experienced programmer, you should not even attempt to interpret these values. The key point is that you know the files are not identical.

DATE Command

DATE lets you change the date in the PC's built-in calendar. Hence, DATE does the same thing in DOS that the DATE$ statement does in BASIC.

The DATE command displays the following prompt:

```
Current date is day mm-dd-yy
Enter new date:
```

To change the date, enter a one- or two-digit month (1 to 12), a one- or two-digit day (1 to 31), and a two- or four-digit year. If the year is a two-digit number, the PC automatically precedes it with 19. DATE accepts two-digit years from 80 to 99 and four-digit years from 1980 to 2099.

DISKCOMP (Disk Compare) Command

DISKCOMP is like COMP, except that it compares entire disks, rather than just files. Generally, you run DISKCOMP after DISKCOPY, to verify the copy. You can use DISKCOMP with either one or two disk drives.

DISKCOMP with One Drive. If you have only one disk drive, enter

```
DISKCOMP
```

The screen shows

```
Insert first diskette in drive A
Strike any key when ready
```

Put your first disk in drive A and press the space bar. DISKCOMP displays

```
Comparing 1 side(s)
```

It then gives the prompt

```
Insert second diskette in drive A
Strike any key when ready
```

If the disks are identical, DISKCOMP returns to the first prompt message, ready for you to compare more disks. If the disks are different, DISKCOMP tells you which tracks are unalike, with messages such as

```
Compare error(s) on track 10
```

DISKCOMP with Two Drives. If you have two disk drives, enter

DISKCOMP B: (If drive A is active)

or

DISKCOMP A: (If drive B is active)

The prompts and results are like those you get with a one-drive system.

SYS (System) Command

SYS copies the operating system files from the active drive to the specified drive. By operating system files we mean the ones you get when you FORMAT a disk with the /S option: COPY, DATE, DIR, ERASE, RENAME, TIME, and TYPE.

SYS has the general form

```
SYS d:
```

where *d:* is the drive you are copying to.

Essentially, SYS does the same thing as FORMAT's /S option but without affecting the files already on the disk. You normally use SYS to transfer DOS onto a program disk that requires it but is sold without it.

Incidentally, the disk you are transferring *to* must already be formatted with a FORMAT d: /S command, so it is prepared to receive these new files!

TIME Command

TIME lets you change the time on the PC's built-in clock. TIME thereby does the same thing in DOS that the TIME$ statement does in BASIC.

TIME displays the following prompt:

```
Current time is hh:mm:ss.xx
Enter new time:
```

where *hh* is the hours count (0–23), *mm* is the minutes count (0–59), *ss* is the seconds count (0–59), and xx is the hundredths of seconds count (0–99).

To leave the time as it is, press Enter. Otherwise, you may change any count you want. Just remember to precede the minutes and seconds values with a colon and the hundredths of seconds value with a period.

For example, to change the time to 4:10:00.00, proceed as follows:

```
TIME
Current time is 12:13:46.17
Enter new time: 4:10
```

Since you omitted the seconds and hundredths of seconds counts, the computer makes them both zero.

Final Comments About DOS

This completes our discussion of DOS. Admittedly, the term "disk operating system" is rather forbidding. It sounds like something only a computer expert could understand. But as you now know, DOS is just a set of commands that lets you manage information on disks.

DOS lets you add, delete, copy, and compare files. It also lets you format a disk (prepare it for use) and make backup copies of disks. In all, DOS frees you from the drudgery of manipulating disk files and gives you more time to do useful work or play games. Although DOS is not exciting, you must have a working knowledge of it to use your computer efficiently.

4.4 DOS PROGRAMS USED WITH ASSEMBLY LANGUAGE

This final section describes DOS programs used to prepare *assembly language* programs. If you intend to use only BASIC (a good idea if you are a beginner), you need not understand these programs. Still, you may want to read about them and learn what assembly language is and why it is used.

BASIC's Drawbacks

If you have never programmed before, you were probably surprised to learn how easy BASIC programming is. You can learn to write short BASIC programs quickly and without much effort. BASIC is easy to learn because it has a small, simple vocabulary of English-like words and phrases. Thus, most beginners do all their programming in BASIC.

The obvious question is, "Why use anything else?" One reason is that BASIC, like human languages, is not well suited to everything. Some tasks are much easier in other languages; imagine, for example, trying to describe fine cooking without some French words or symphonies without some Italian terms. Similarly, special computing tasks such as graphics, music, or word processing are often easier in special languages or modified versions of BASIC.

Furthermore, BASIC is quite slow. The term "slow" may surprise the beginner, since short programs run instantaneously. However, problems occur in the following situations:

1. *When large amounts of data are involved.* You will notice how slow BASIC is when a program must, for example, sort a long list of names and addresses or accounts. Similarly, BASIC will be quite slow when a program must search through a 50-page report or keep inventory records on thousands of items.
2. *When graphics are involved.* If a program is drawing a picture on the screen, it must work quickly or the delay will be intolerable. If objects in the picture are supposed to move, the program must be fast enough to make the motion look natural. This is particularly difficult when the picture contains many objects (such as spaceships, base stations, and alien invaders), all of which are moving in different directions.
3. *When a lot of decisions or "thinking" is required.* This is often necessary in complex games like checkers or chess. The program has to try many possibilities and decide on a reasonable move. Obviously, the more possibilities there are and the more analysis is required, the longer it will take the computer to move.

Why is BASIC slow? In the first place, the computer actually translates each BASIC statement into simple internal commands (so-called "machine" or "assembly" language). It does this every time it runs the BASIC program. Thus, much of the computer's time is spent translating the program, not running it.

There are versions of BASIC (called *compilers*) that perform the translation once and then save the translated version. However, BASIC would still be slow because of its mechanical nature. It is really like an automobile with an automatic transmission; no amount of coaxing can ever get you the performance or fuel economy that a skillful driver can achieve with a manual transmission. The human being is simply a more flexible, more skillful, and smarter operator than is the automatic transmission or the BASIC interpreter or compiler.

Assembly language is the computer equivalent of a manual transmission. It gives the programmer greater control over the computer at the cost of more work, more detail, and less convenience. Like an automatic transmission, BASIC is good enough most of the time for most programmers. But for those who must get maximum performance from their computers (like professional race drivers), assembly language is essential. You will find that most complex games, graphics programs, and large business programs are written at least partially in assembly language.

What is Assembly Language?

Like BASIC, assembly language is a set of words that tells the computer what to do. However, the words in the assembly language instruction set refer to computer components directly. It is like the difference between telling someone to walk down to the corner and telling them precisely how to move their muscles and maneuver past obstacles. Obviously, a simple command is sufficient most of the time; only athletes or mountain climbers need the more detailed instructions.

Assembly language programs give the computer detailed commands such as "load 32 into the AX register," "transfer the contents of the CL register into the DL register," and "store the number in the DL register into memory location 3456." As you see, BASIC and assembly language differ in how you instruct the computer. *With BASIC, you speak in generalities; with assembly language, you speak in specifics.*

Although assembly language programs take more time and effort to write than do BASIC programs, they also run much faster. The level of detail is the key here. The idea is the same as an athlete who runs faster or jumps farther by watching every step of what he or she does. Precise form is essential to achieving maximum performance.

Developing an Assembly Language Program

Although assembly language programs look quite different from BASIC programs, you follow the same procedures to develop them. However, in assembly language the *mechanics* are more involved. There are seven steps in developing an assembly language program:

1. Define the task and design the program. This often involves drawing a *flow chart*, a "blueprint" of how the program operates.

2. Write the program instructions on paper.
3. Type the written program into the computer using an *editor*.
4. Assemble the program using an *assembler*. If the assembler finds errors, correct them with the editor and reassemble the program.
5. Convert the assembler output to a "run module" using the *linker*.
6. Execute (run) the program.
7. Check the results. If they differ from what you expected, you must find the errors or "bugs"; that is, you must "debug" the program.

If your program is short and simple, you should be able to perform these steps quickly. However, longer and more complex programs will require more time on each step, especially defining the problem itself.

Editor (EDLIN). Step 3 refers to an editor. This is a program that lets you enter and prepare your program. We call your readable version of the program the *source program*.

IBM's editor program, EDLIN, is on the DOS disk. EDLIN is a line editor; that is, its commands operate on numbered lines in your program. Table 4-4 summarizes the most useful EDLIN commands.

Assembler. The computer cannot directly execute the program you prepare using EDLIN. An assembler must convert that source program into an *object program* the computer can understand.

Linker (LINK). The IBM DOS can store a program at any convenient place in memory. However, to use this feature, you must convert the assembled program to a form that can be moved around (the computer term is *relocatable*) using a program called LINK. LINK is also on the DOS disk.

The IBM literature refers to an assembled program as an *object module* and to a relocatable object program as a *run module*. Hence, LINK's job is to create a run module from an object module. LINK also allows you to combine several object modules (perhaps including old programs or ones copied from books or magazines) into one large-run module.

A Debugging Program (DEBUG). You can run your completed program in two ways:

TABLE 4-4. COMMON EDLIN COMMANDS

Command	*Action*	*Comments*
A	Adds lines from the keyboard to the end of program in memory.	Use this command to create a new source program.
line D or line,line D	Deletes lines.	
line	Displays a line for editing.	
E	Saves the edited program on disk and then returns to DOS.	Use this command to end an editing session. See also Q.
line I	Inserts lines from the keyboard ahead of the specified program line.	
line L or line,line D	Lists lines.	
Q	Returns to DOS without saving any editing changes.	See also E.
line,line Rstring1 then ⟨F6⟩string2	Replaces all occurrences of string1 with string2 within the specified range.	
line,line Sstring	Searches for the specified string.	

1. You can simply enter its name from DOS.
2. You can run it under the control of the DEBUG program.

Generally, you only run a program from DOS when you are sure it has no mistakes. Until then, you run it under DEBUG.

The DEBUG program (on the DOS disk) lets you control your program as it runs. Among other things, DEBUG lets you change and display values, stop your program at a particular point, or run your program one step at a time. DEBUG thus provides you with tools that help in identifying and correcting errors in programs. Table 4-5 summarizes common DEBUG commands.

TABLE 4-5. COMMON DEBUG COMMANDS

Command	*Action*	*Comments*
D address or D start-address end-address	Displays the contents of memory locations.	
E address value	Changes the contents of a memory location.	
F start-address L bytes value	Fills a block of memory with a specified value.	
G [address]*	Executes a program. If you include address, the computer stops before executing that instruction and displays registers.	See also T.
Q	Ends DEBUG and returns to DOS.	
R [register-name]	Displays contents of one or all registers.	If you display just one register, R allows you to change its contents.
S start-address [end-address] value	Searches memory for a specified value.	
T [instruction-count]	Executes one or more instructions and displays register values with each.	See also G.

* Brackets indicate that the item(s) inside them are optional.

Chapter 5

SOUND, GRAPHICS, AND COLOR

The IBM PC has extensive sound and picture-making (*graphics*) capabilities. Actually, the lack of inexpensive input and output devices has long limited computers to dealing with cards and typed input and to producing huge stacks of numbers as output. There is no inherent reason why a computer cannot deal with sounds, pictures, and colors as well as it handles numbers. Not only do such capabilities make for better games, but they also provide more natural and more effective communications in serious applications for business, engineering, education, finance, and science.

This chapter covers those BASIC statements in three groups: sound, graphics, and color. Although graphics and color are related, we treat them separately to avoid overwhelming you with information.

5.1 SOUND STATEMENTS

The PC has two sound-making statements, SOUND and PLAY. Both generate sounds through the speaker. SOUND produces a single note, whereas PLAY produces a series of notes that can form a tune. All three BASICs have SOUND, but only Advanced BASIC (BASICA) has PLAY.

SOUND Statement

SOUND has two parameters. The first is the note's frequency in Hertz (cycles per second). For reference purposes, Figure 5-1 shows the frequencies for the various notes on a piano. (SOUND accepts only whole number frequencies, however, so you would have to approximate these notes.) The second parameter is how long the note lasts in "clock ticks." The PC produces 18.2 clock ticks per second or about one every

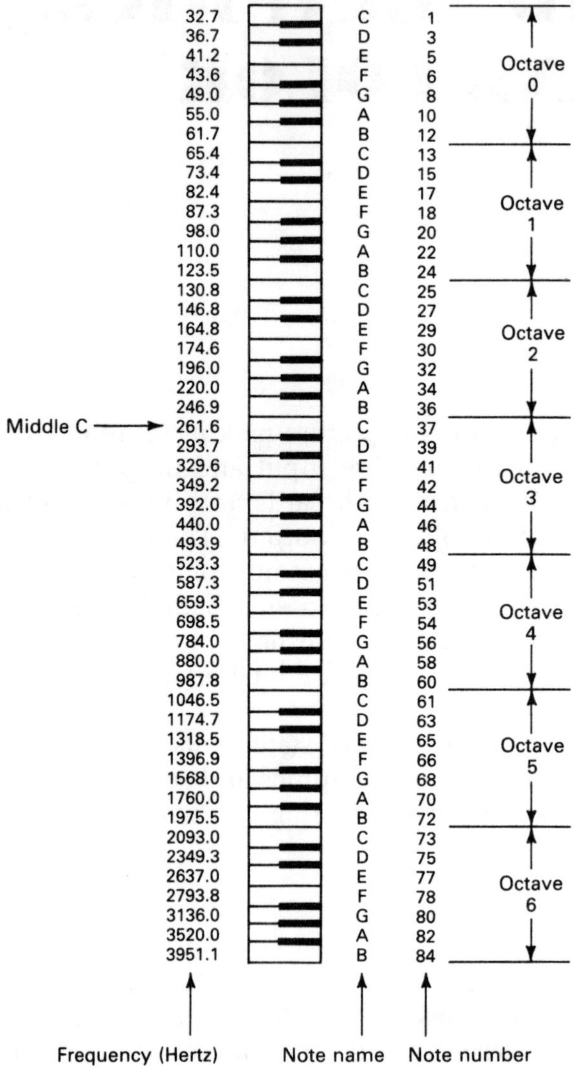

Figure 5-1. Musical notes for use in PLAY statements

TABLE 5-1. SOME TIME VALUES IN PC CLOCK TICKS

Time (seconds)	*Duration (clock ticks)*
$\frac{1}{10}$	2
$\frac{1}{5}$	4
$\frac{1}{4}$	5
$\frac{1}{3}$	6
$\frac{1}{2}$	9
$\frac{2}{3}$	12
$\frac{3}{4}$	14
1	18
$1\frac{1}{4}$	23
$1\frac{1}{2}$	27
$1\frac{3}{4}$	32
2	36

.055 seconds. Table 5-1 gives clock tick values corresponding to some commonly used times.

The frequency can lie anywhere between 37 and 32,767 Hertz. Humans can usually hear up to 20,000 Hertz. The PC will still have an audience, however, if you have a dog, since dogs can hear high-frequency sounds. The lower limit, 37 Hertz, is roughly the lowest note that can be played on a bass viol. The note may last anywhere from 0 (a rest) to 65,535 clock ticks (about 1 hour).

For example,

```
SOUND 262,5
```

produces a tone with a frequency of 262 Hz (just above middle C on a piano) that last 5 clock ticks or one-fourth of a second.

The problem with SOUND is that you must specify the frequency and duration of each note you want the computer to play. That is all right if your program just emits a few squeaks or beeps occasionally, but to create music you need Advanced BASIC's PLAY statement.

PLAY Statement

PLAY makes the PC act like a computerized music box: it plays a sequence of notes provided in a special character string.

PLAY can play 84 different notes, seven complete octaves. Figure 5-1 shows these notes superimposed on a standard piano keyboard. If you are a musician, you will notice that only the two lowest keys (A and A♯) and the two highest keys (C and C♯) are missing. Furthermore, PLAY lets you select notes either by name (for instance, G or C#) or by number (1 to 84). Either way, you need not specify a note's frequency, as you must with SOUND.

PLAY requires a string, a sequence of special commands that tells the computer which notes to play. Table 5-2 divides these commands into three groups: note commands, style and tempo commands, and foreground and background commands.

Note Commands. You must tell PLAY the name or number and duration of every note. Notes have the same names as in formal music. That is, the *natural notes* (the white keys on the piano) are A through G. The *sharps* and *flats* (the black keys) are also A through G, with the addition of "#" (for sharp) or "−" (for flat). For example, D# means D sharp and D− means D flat.

If you refer to notes by name, you must also specify their *octave*. As Figure 5-1 shows, PLAY's 84 notes are divided into seven octaves (0 through 6), each of which goes from C to B (C-D-E-F-G-A-B). To select an octave, you precede the note names with an O command. Once you select the octave, it remains in force until the next O command.

For example, the statement

```
10 PLAY "O3FGAFFGAF"
```

plays the first eight notes (F-G-A-F-F-G-A-F) of a familiar tune in octave 3. Since the string contains no L (length) command, the computer makes each note a *quarter note*.

You may also specify notes by numbers between 0 and 84, where 0 means *rest*. The command that does this, N (number), is convenient if you want to play a few notes from another octave. For example,

```
20 PLAY "AA#N49AA#N49"
```

continues the preceding tune in octave 3, but momentarily jumps into octave 4 to play note 49 (C). Using N49 saves us from having to put the longer sequence *O4CO3* in the PLAY string.

If you want anything except quarter notes, you must tell PLAY how long they should last. The L (length) command has the general form L*n*, where *n* is the length of the note. PLAY uses *n* as a divisor, so L1 selects a whole note, L2 a half note, and L4 a quarter note. *n* may range from 1 to 64, so you can play 64th notes.

The L command sets the length of every note that follows it in the string. To set the length of an individual note, just attach an *n* value to

TABLE 5-2. MUSIC-PLAYING COMMANDS IN A PLAY STATEMENT

Command	*Action*	*Comments*
	Note Commands	
A to G *for natural notes* A# to G# *for sharps* A− to G− *for flats*	Plays note specified by letter, with optional sharp (#) or flat (−) suffix.	O command selects octave.
L*n*	Sets length of a note; *n* may range from 1 to 64.	L1 is a whole note, L2 is a half note, L4 is a quarter note, and so on.
N*n*	Plays note *n*, where *n* may range from 0 to 84. $n = 0$ means rest (no note).	Figure 5-1 identifies the notes.
O*n*	Sets current octave. There are seven octaves, from 0 to 6.	Figure 5-1 identifies the octaves.
P*n*	Pauses (rests) for a note value, where *n* may range from 1 to 64.	P1 rests for a whole note, P2 for a half note, P4 for a quarter note, and so on.
	Style and Tempo Commands	
MN	Music normal. Each note plays seven-eights of the period set by L.	
ML	Music legato. Each note plays the full period set by L.	
MS	Music staccato. Each note plays three-fourths of the period set by L.	
T*n*	Tempo. Sets the number of quarter notes in a minute, from 32 to 255.	If you omit T, music plays at 120 quarter notes per minute.
	Foreground and Background Commands	
MF	Music foreground. BASIC program waits for PLAY or SOUND to complete before continuing.	This is the default state.
MB	Music background. BASIC program continues to execute while music created by PLAY or SOUND runs in the background.	The PC can store up to 32 notes to run in the background.

its name. For instance, A16 makes A a sixteenth note, but does not affect the length of subsequent notes, as L16A does.

To hear the effect of the L command, vary the length of the notes in the preceding example by rewriting line 10 as

```
10 PLAY "L8O3FGAFFGAF"
```

Here, L8 makes every note an eighth note instead of a quarter note.

Finally, the P (pause) command puts a pause (or rest) between notes in the music. This command has the general form P*n*, where *n* may range from 1 to 64. The length of a pause is the same as length of a note. Hence, P1 pauses for a whole note, P2 for a half note, and P4 for a quarter note.

Clearly, the PC has significant music-making capabilities. If you have formal music training, you should have no trouble transcribing or creating music. If you lack formal training (even if you are mostly tone-deaf), you can still experiment until you get the sound you want.

Style and Tempo Commands. These commands play the role of an orchestra conductor; they set the speed of the music and the way the PC interprets the score (the PLAY string). Like L and O, they affect every note that follows them.

T (tempo), the most useful of these commands, sets the rate at which the PC plays music. Its general form is T*n*, where *n* is the number of quarter notes in a minute. The value *n* may range from 32 to 255. T32 holds a quarter note for nearly 2 seconds while T255 holds it for less than a quarter of a second. The default (no T command) is T120, which holds whole notes for about half a second.

The other three commands, MN, ML, and MS, change the way in which PLAY interprets notes. MN (music normal) holds each note seven-eighths of the time set by L (length). That is, it cuts off the last eighth of every note and simply rests during that period.

Similarly, MS (music staccato) holds each note three-fourths of the time set by L. This cuts off the last one-fourth of every note, producing a crisp, abrupt sound. The final command, ML (music legato), turns off MN or MS and makes PLAY once again hold notes for the full L time, with no rests.

The following sequence plays the natural notes in octave 4 at a tempo of 100 with MN, then with MS, and finally with ML:

```
10 PLAY "O4T100" ' Octave is 4, tempo is 100
20 PLAY "MNCDEFGAB" ' Chop notes to 7/8
30 PLAY "MSCDEFGAB" ' Chop notes to 3/4
40 PLAY "MLCDEFGAB" ' Give all notes full value
```

Foreground and Background Commands. In programs that use both sound *and* graphics (such as video games and instructional programs), we want music to play while the screen displays pictures. To provide this capability, IBM BASIC has a command that plays a series of notes stored in memory at the same time the computer is executing other instructions.

This command, MB (music background), stores a PLAY string of up to 32 notes inside the computer and then turns on a special circuit that plays those notes. As soon as that circuit is turned on, the computer continues to the next line in the program.

You might want to run this simple program, which displays numbers while the computer plays the natural notes in octave 4:

```
10 PLAY "O4MBCDEFGAB"
20 FOR J = 1 TO 30
30 PRINT J
40 NEXT J
```

MB's opposite, MF (music foreground), makes the computer wait until the PLAY statement ends. Unless you enter MB, the computer always plays music in the foreground manner.

Dotted Notes. In formal music, a dot beside a note tells you to hold it 50 percent longer than usual. You hold a dotted half note for the length of three quarter notes, a dotted quarter note for the length of three eighth notes, and so on.

To dot a note in the PLAY string, simply follow it with a period. Dotting a note is a form of musical shorthand. For example, we can write "A4." instead of "A4A8".

PLAYing with String Variables. Besides note names and numbers, the PLAY string may also include string variables. By defining a note sequence as a string variable, you can repeat a part of a tune any time you need it.

To include a string variable in PLAY, precede its name with X. The X tells BASIC to execute the string. For instance, in "Mary Had a Little Lamb," the first four notes are repeated in the second line. To save time and effort, you could program the PC to play the tune as follows:

```
10 A$ = "EDCD" ' These notes are repeated
20 PLAY "MST200" ' Play staccato at tempo 200
30 PLAY "XA$;EEE2DDD2EGG2" ' First line
40 PLAY "XA$;EEEEDDEDC1" ' Second line
```

Since the PC has only one speaker, you cannot create two-part harmony. That is one of the PC's few limitations. Of course, other manufacturers do offer additional hardware that can expand the PC's musical capabilities.

5.2 GRAPHICS STATEMENTS

Until now, you have been using the PC to display only letters, numbers, and other characters. In IBM terminology, you have operated the PC in the *text mode*.

Besides the normal keyboard characters, the PC has a variety of *block graphics characters* that let you construct simple (but rather primitive-looking) pictures on the screen. This section describes how to create such pictures.

If you have IBM's Monochrome Display, you are limited to drawing pictures in the text mode. However, if you have a color display or a television set (either black-and-white or color), the computer has an IBM Color/Graphics Monitor Adapter. This lets you draw sophisticated, detailed pictures on the screen, not just character drawings.

With the Color/Graphics Monitor Adapter, you can switch the computer into its *graphics mode*, in which it displays dots on the screen rather than characters. And if you arrange these dots properly, they form pictures.

If you have a Monochrome Display, you need only to read about text mode graphics. But if you have any other kind of display, you should read the entire section.

Drawing Pictures in Text Mode

In the text mode, the PC's screen is normally divided into 25 lines (rows) of 80 columns. This is the state the computer is in when you turn on the power.

Screen Layout. To the computer, the screen is like a wall of mail boxes in a post office. To display a character at one of the 2000 possible screen locations, you must tell BASIC which character to display and where to display it. We will discuss the characters shortly. For now, let us concentrate on the screen locations.

You tell BASIC where to display a character by specifying row and column numbers. Rows are numbered 1 (top) through 25 (bottom).

Columns are numbered 1 (left) through 80 (right). To refer to a specific location, you give BASIC its coordinates in the form *row,column*. For example, the upper left-hand corner is location (1,1) and the lower right-hand corner is location (25,80). Figure 5-2 shows the screen layout for an 80-column display.

The PC can display 256 different characters, including many that are not on the keyboard. Table 5-3 shows the characters, arranged by the numbers that identify them in BASIC. Besides the keyboard characters, the PC has smiling faces; playing card symbols; mathematical and musical symbols; proofreader's marks; letters used in foreign languages such as Greek, German, and Spanish; and an assortment of arrows, lines, and boxes. To display a character, you simply give BASIC its number from Table 5-3.

Now you know how to specify a character location on the screen and a character number. All you need to find out is how to actually *display* characters.

Text Mode Graphics Statements. To create pictures in the text mode, you need the four BASIC statements in Table 5-4. CLS (clear screen) is straightforward. PRINT is familiar, but the form PRINT CHR$(n) is new.

Quite simply, to display a character in text mode, you only have to move (LOCATE) the cursor to the appropriate position, then PRINT the character. Once the character is on the screen, it stays there until you clear the screen or PRINT another character at that location.

For example, the lines

```
10 CLS                ' Clear the screen
20 LOCATE 12,1        ' Move cursor to row 12, column 1
30 PRINT CHR$(127)    ' Display triangle
```

clear the screen and then display a triangle in the leftmost column of row 12. CLS moves the cursor to the upper left-hand corner (location 1,1), so if you want to display the triangle there, you can omit line 20.

Finding the Current Cursor Position. To draw pictures, your program must be able to find out where the cursor is located at any given time. BASIC has two functions that provide the cursor's location: CSRLIN gives the cursor's vertical (row) position, and POS(0) gives its horizontal (column) position.

To display a character *relative* to the current cursor position, use CSRLIN and POS(0) as the row and column parameters of a LOCATE

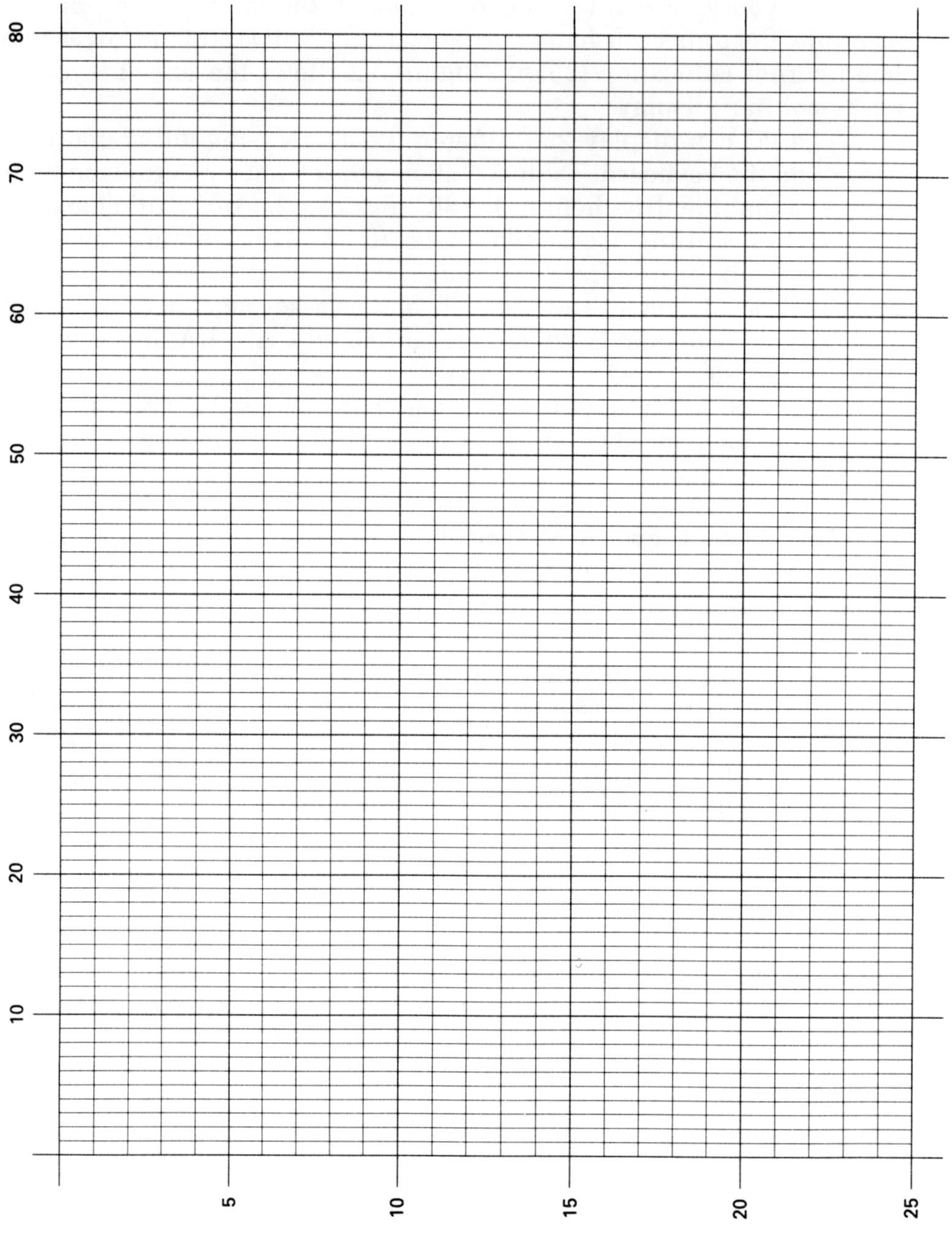

Figure 5-2. Screen layout in text mode (80 columns)

TABLE 5-3. TEXT MODE DISPLAY CHARACTERS

Value	Character	Value	Character	Value	Character	Value	Character
000	(null)	032	(space)	064	@	096	`
001	☺	033	!	065	A	097	a
002	☻	034	"	066	B	098	b
003	♥	035	#	067	C	099	c
004	♦	036	$	068	D	100	d
005	♣	037	%	069	E	101	e
006	♠	038	&	070	F	102	f
007	(beep)	039	'	071	G	103	g
008	◘	040	(	072	H	104	h
009	(tab)	041	)	073	I	105	i
010	(line feed)	042	*	074	J	106	j
011	(home)	043	+	075	K	107	k
012	(form feed)	044	,	076	L	108	l
013	(carriage return)	045	-	077	M	109	m
014	♫	046	.	078	N	110	n
015	☼	047	/	079	O	111	o
016	►	048	0	080	P	112	p
017	◄	049	1	081	Q	113	q
018	↕	050	2	082	R	114	r
019	‼	051	3	083	S	115	s
020	¶	052	4	084	T	116	t
021	§	053	5	085	U	117	u
022	▬	054	6	086	V	118	v
023	↨	055	7	087	W	119	w
024	↑	056	8	088	X	120	x
025	↓	057	9	089	Y	121	y
026	→	058	:	090	Z	122	z
027	←	059	;	091	[	123	{
028	(cursor right)	060	<	092	\	124	¦
029	(cursor left)	061	=	093	]	125	}
030	(cursor up)	062	>	094	^	126	~
031	(cursor down)	063	?	095	_	127	⌂

Courtesy of IBM Corporation.

TABLE 5-3. (continued)

Value	*Character*	*Value*	*Character*	*Value*	*Character*	*Value*	*Character*
128	Ç	160	á	192	└	224	α
129	ü	161	í	193	┴	225	β
130	é	162	ó	194	┬	226	Γ
131	â	163	ú	195	├	227	π
132	ä	164	ñ	196	─	228	Σ
133	à	165	Ñ	197	┼	229	σ
134	å	166	ª	198	╞	230	µ
135	ç	167	º	199	╟	231	τ
136	ê	168	¿	200	╚	232	Φ
137	ë	169	⌐	201	╔	233	θ
138	è	170	¬	202	╩	234	Ω
139	ï	171	½	203	╦	235	δ
140	î	172	¼	204	╠	236	∞
141	ì	173	¡	205	═	237	Ø
142	Ä	174	«	206	╬	238	∈
143	Å	175	»	207	╧	239	∩
144	É	176	░	208	╨	240	≡
145	æ	177	▒	209	╤	241	±
146	Æ	178	▓	210	╥	242	≥
147	ô	179	│	211	╙	243	≤
148	ö	180	┤	212	╘	244	⌠
149	ò	181	╡	213	╒	245	⌡
150	û	182	╢	214	╓	246	÷
151	ù	183	╖	215	╫	247	≈
152	ÿ	184	╕	216	╪	248	°
153	Ö	185	╣	217	┘	249	•
154	Ü	186	║	218	┌	250	·
155	¢	187	╗	219	█	251	√
156	£	188	╝	220	▄	252	ⁿ
157	¥	189	╜	221	▌	253	²
158	Pt	190	╛	222	▐	254	■
159	ƒ	191	┐	223	▀	255	(blank 'FF')

TABLE 5-4. TEXT MODE GRAPHICS STATEMENTS*

Statement	*Action*	*Comments*
CLS	Clears the screen and starts the cursor in the upper left-hand corner (row 1, column 1).	
LOCATE [row][,col]	Moves the cursor to the specified row and column.	
PRINT CHR$(n)	Displays character *n*.	
SCREEN 0[,[burst][,[apage][,vpage]]]	Sets the screen attributes for subsequent statements.	Only meaningful with the Color/Graphics Monitor Adapter.

* Brackets indicate that the item(s) inside them are optional.

statement. For example,

```
20 LOCATE CSRLIN+1,POS(0)+2
```

moves the cursor one row down and two columns to the right. If the cursor starts at row 10 and column 20, it will end up at row 11 and column 22.

If you try to move the cursor to a row or column position that is off the screen (as, for example, with LOCATE 26,1), the PC will show the error message

```
Illegal function call in line n
```

where *n* is the line number of LOCATE.

SCREEN Statement. The Color/Graphics Monitor Adapter can store up to four 80-column text mode "pages" in its memory. To display a page on the screen, you just tell BASIC which page is the *visual page*. A SCREEN statement switches from one page to another.

SCREEN has the general form

```
SCREEN 0[,[burst][,[apage][,vpage]]]
```

where *burst* turns the color on (burst=1) or off (burst=0), *apage* selects the active page (the page you are sending PRINT commands to), and *vpage* selects the visual page (the page the PC is to display).

Both *apage* and *vpage* can range from 0 to 3 for 80-column displays. When you enter BASIC, the PC sets them to 0.

Note that *burst*, *apage*, and *vpage* are all optional. You can change one, two, or all three with a single SCREEN statement, as these examples show:

```
10 SCREEN 0,1,0,0          ' Turn on color, active and visual page
                             ' are 0
20 SCREEN 0,,,3            ' Display page 3 on the screen
30 SCREEN 0,,2             ' Make page 2 the active page
40 SCREEN 0,0              ' Turn off color
```

Drawing Pictures in Graphics Mode

In the graphics mode, the PC divides the screen into a much denser grid than the normal 25-by-80 text mode grid. (If the text mode screen is like a wall covered with mail boxes, the graphics mode screen is like a honeycomb!) And instead of displaying characters in the grid, the PC displays *dots*.

Medium Resolution and High Resolution. The graphics mode has two possible dot grids. IBM calls these *medium resolution* and *high resolution*.

In medium resolution, the PC divides the screen into 320 horizontal positions by 200 vertical positions and displays dots in color. In high resolution, the PC divides the screen into 640 horizontal positions by 200 vertical positions and displays dots in black and white. Positions on a graphics mode screen are called *points*.

Screen Layout. Unlike the text mode, where character positions are numbered starting at 1, points on a graphics screen are numbered starting at 0. Hence, the upper left-hand corner is point (0,0) and the lower right-hand corner is point (319,199) for medium resolution or (639,199) for high resolution. Figure 5-3 shows the screen layout for medium-resolution graphics.

Graphics Mode Statements. Table 5-5 lists the nine statements used in the graphics mode. Some have color options that we will discuss later. Table 5-5 divides the statements into three groups: general purpose, line and figure drawing, and dot display.

The general-purpose statements are straightforward. SCREEN switches the PC from text mode to graphics mode. SCREEN 1 puts the PC in medium resolution, while SCREEN 2 puts it in high resolution. CLS, as usual, clears the screen. Note, however, that CLS starts the cursor in the center of the screen in the graphics mode, not in the upper left-hand corner.

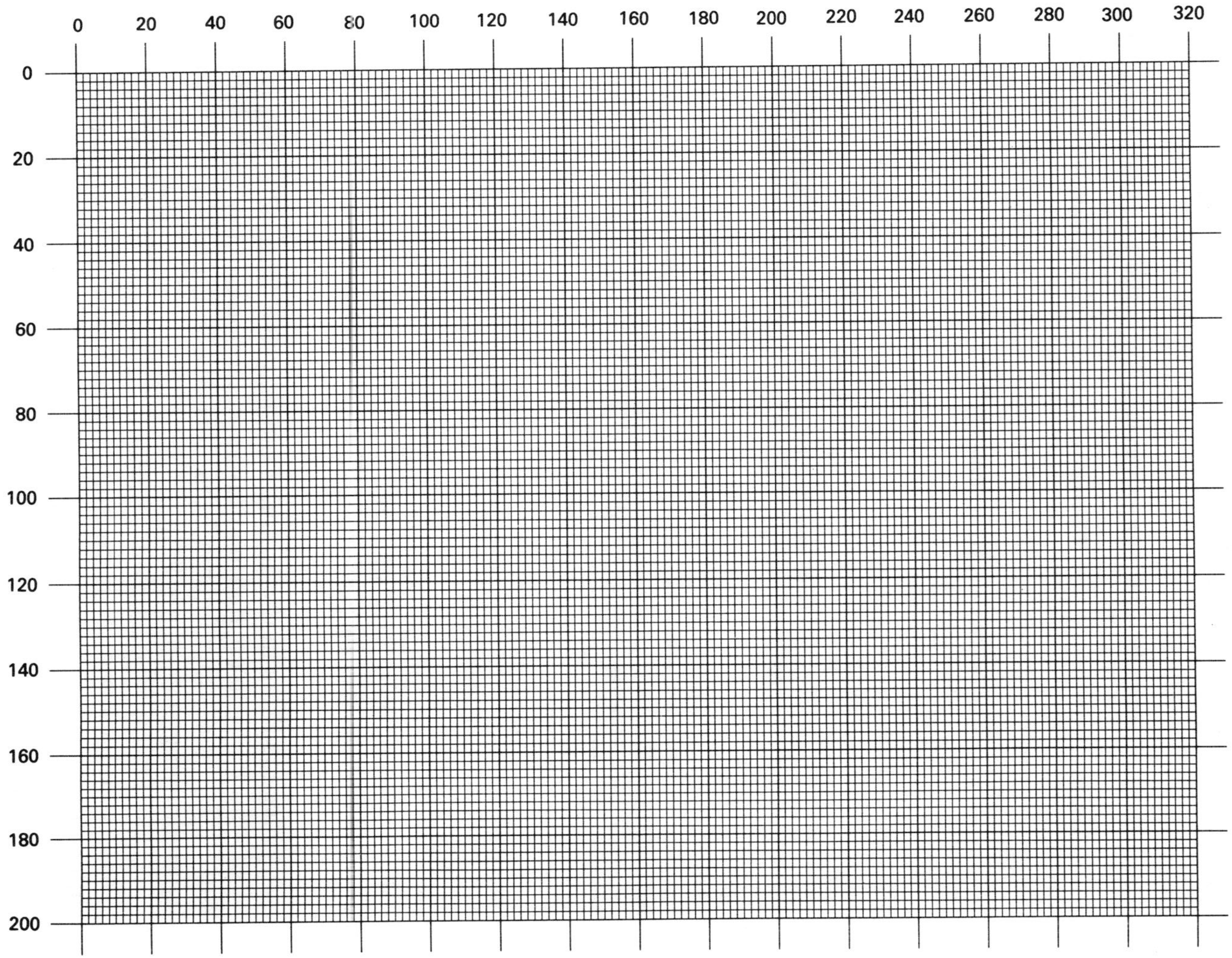

Figure 5-3. Screen layout for medium-resolution graphics

TABLE 5-5. GRAPHICS MODE STATEMENTS*

Statement	*Action*	*Comments*
CLS	Clears the screen and starts cursor in the center.	Note the different starting place in graphics mode; center rather than upper left-hand corner.
SCREEN 1 or SCREEN 2	Selects medium- (1) or high- (2) resolution graphics.	
	Line- and Figure-Drawing Statements	
CIRCLE (xcenter,ycenter),radius[,,start,end]	Draws a circle or an arc.	Advanced BASIC only.
DRAW string	Draws an object specified by a string.	Advanced BASIC only.
LINE [(x1,y1)]-(x2,y2) or LINE (x1,y1)-(x2,y2),,B	Draws a line or a box.	B option selects a box.
PSET (x,y)	Creates a reference point.	
	Dot Display Statements	
GET (x1,y1)-(x2,y2),array	Reads graphics points into an array.	Opposite of PUT.
PRESET (x,y)	Erases a point.	
PUT (x1,y1),array	Writes graphics points from an array onto an area of the screen.	Opposite of GET.

* Brackets indicate that the item(s) inside them are optional.

Once the PC is in the graphics mode, you can use CIRCLE, DRAW, LINE, and PSET to create line drawings. Or you can use GET, PRESET, and PUT to construct figures from dots. We will discuss the line- and figure-drawing statements first.

CIRCLE, quite reasonably, draws a circle. Its center is at (*xcenter, ycenter*) and its radius is *radius* graphics points. For example, the statements

```
50 SCREEN 1
60 CIRCLE (160,100),10
```

draw a circle with a radius of 10 points around point (160,100) on a medium-resolution screen.

The option *start,end* lets you draw just a portion of a circle: an arc. The two parts of this option, *start* and *end*, are angles expressed in radians. Since there are two π radians in a circle ($\pi = 3.141593$), *start* and *end* may range from 0 to 2 times π. If you view the circle as the face of a clock, 0 is at 3 o'clock and the values increase counterclockwise. As Figure 5-4 shows, PI/2 is at 12 o'clock, PI is at 9 o'clock, 3*PI/2 is at 6 o'clock, and 2*PI is back at the 3 o'clock (or 0) position.

If you give *start* and *end* positive values, CIRCLE will draw just the arc. If you give them negative values, the PC will connect the arc to the circle's centerpoint, thereby drawing a slice of a piechart or a circle with a wedge removed (depending on how big the arc is). For example, the statements

```
100 PI = 3.141593
110 SCREEN 1
120 CIRCLE (160,100),60,,-PI/2,-3*PI/2
```

will draw the left half of a circle. By multiplying PI by the proper factors, you can create circle segments as wide or as narrow as you want.

LINE draws a line or a box. LINE has three different forms. The simplest form,

```
LINE -(x,y)
```

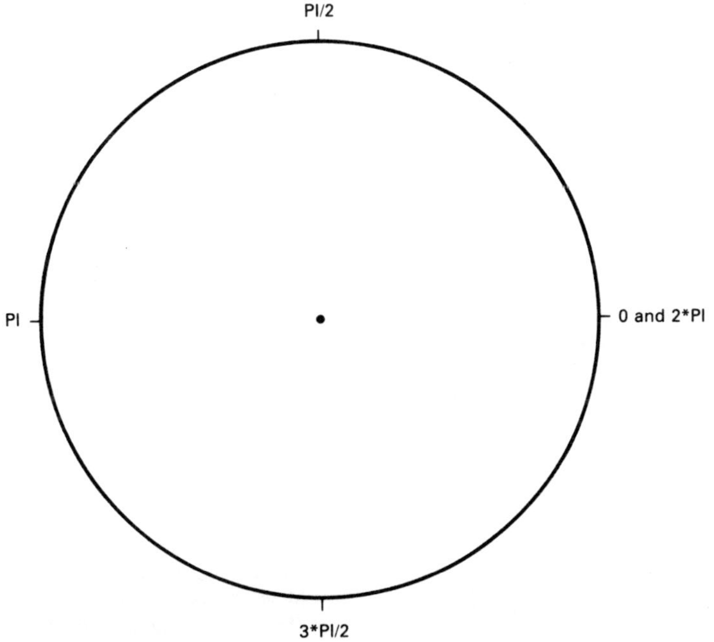

Figure 5-4. Quarter points on a circle

draws a line between the last point you referenced and point (x,y). Hence, the statements

```
50 SCREEN 1
60 CIRCLE (160,10),10
70 LINE -(170,100)
```

draw a circle and then connect a horizontal line from the center of the circle to its right edge.

You can start the line anywhere by using the form

```
LINE (x1,y1)-(x2,y2)
```

Here, the line extends from point (x1,y1) to point (x2,y2).

Finally, you can draw a box by using the form

```
LINE (x1,y1)-(x2,y2),,B
```

The upper left-hand corner of the box is at (x1,y1), and its lower right-hand corner is at (x2,y2). For example,

```
80 LINE (0,0)-(99,149),,B
```

draws a rectangle 100 points wide (remember, the coordinates start at 0 rather than at 1) and 150 points high in the upper left-hand corner of the screen.

The DRAW statement is to graphics what PLAY is to sound. Just as PLAY plays a tune based on a string of note commands, DRAW draws a figure based on a string of movement commands. Each movement command draws a line from the current screen position to another point. Table 5-6 summarizes these commands. In each case, *n* determines how long the line is.

You construct a DRAW string from a series of movement com-

TABLE 5-6. DRAW STATEMENT'S MOVEMENT COMMANDS

Command	*Meaning*
U*n*	Move up.
D*n*	Move down.
L*n*	Move left.
R*n*	Move right.
E*n*	Move diagonally up and right.
F*n*	Move diagonally down and right.
G*n*	Move diagonally down and left.
H*n*	Move diagonally up and left.

mands separated by a space. For example, the following DRAW statement draws a hexagon with sides 20 points long:

```
100 DRAW "E20 R20 F20 G20 L20 H20"
```

Figure 5-5 shows how each of these commands contributes to the hexagon.

Where does the hexagon appear? It starts at whatever point you referenced last. For instance, if the computer just executed a CIRCLE statement that drew a circle around (160,100), the hexagon will start at (160,100).

If you want DRAW to start at some place other than the current position, use PSET to change the reference point. For example, to start the hexagon at (170,90), enter

```
90 PSET (170,90)
100 DRAW "E20 R20 F20 G20 L20 H20"
```

You might think of PSET as the graphics mode equivalent of the text mode's LOCATE statement.

Just as the PLAY statement has options besides the note commands, the DRAW statement has options besides the movement commands. For instance, you can apply two prefixes. B performs the move but does not draw a line. (This is convenient for drawing two separate figures with a single DRAW statement.) N performs the move (and draws the line) but then returns to the starting position.

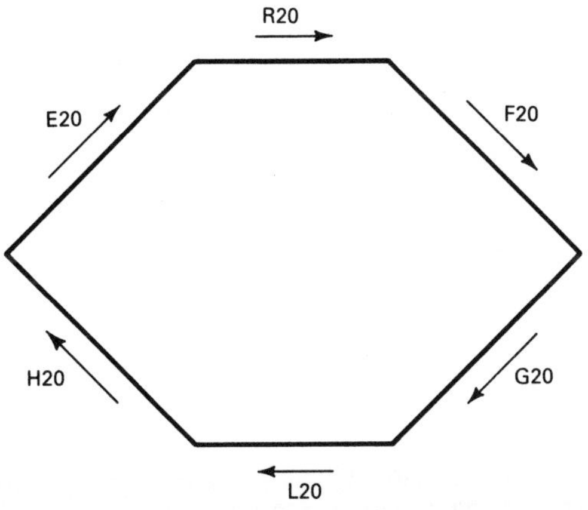

Figure 5-5. Example figure (a hexagon) drawn with a DRAW statement

The following statement uses both prefixes:

```
200 DRAW "BR30 E40 F40 G40 NH40"
```

Here, the PC moves right 30 points from the current position (BR30) and then draws a diamond-shaped figure. E40, F40, and G40 draw the upper left, upper right, and lower right sides of the diamond. NH40 completes the diamond by drawing its lower left side and then returns to the beginning of the line. Hence, the next DRAW statement will start at the bottom of the diamond.

The preceding DRAW commands are convenient for drawing simple figures, but they all require you to know the length of each line you want to draw. A more powerful command, move (M), lets you draw a line from the current position to any other point on the screen. M has three forms:

1. *M x,y* draws a line to point (x,y).
2. *M +x,y* adds x to the current horizontal coordinate and y to the current vertical coordinate and then draws a line to the calculated point.
3. *M −x,y* subtracts x from the current horizontal coordinate and y from the current vertical coordinate and then draws a line to the calculated point.

For example, if the PC is at point (160,100), *M 150,90* draws a line to (150,90), *M +20,10* draws a line to (180,110), and *M −20,10* draws a line to (140,90).

DRAW also allows you to change the size or scale of a figure. With the S command, you can DRAW a figure double size at one place and half size at another place.

The S command has the form Sn, where n may range from 1 to 255. DRAW always divides n by 4, so S8 draws a figure at twice its normal size while S2 draws a figure at half its normal size.

To see how S works, assume that we want to draw our earlier diamond shape at two places on the screen. We will draw it twice normal size at point (160,100) and half normal size at (80,60). Since we need the same DRAW statement twice, we will give its string a name. This sequence does the job:

```
100 A$ = "E40 F40 G40 H40" ' Commands to draw a diamond
110 PSET (160,100) ' Start at (160,100)
120 DRAW "S8"     ' Scale = 2
```

```
130 DRAW A$         ' Draw double-size diamond
140 PSET (80,60)    ' Next diamond is at (80,60)
150 DRAW "S2"       ' Scale = 1/2
160 DRAW A$         ' Draw half-size diamond
```

By naming DRAW strings, you can build a collection of shapes for your program to use. And since S can range from S1 to S255, you can draw any shape as small as one-fourth size and as large as 64 times normal size.

If you are not satisfied with line drawings, you can construct drawings from dots with PSET and the *dot display statements* GET, PRESET, and PUT. PRESET is similar to PSET, but PSET displays a dot at the specified coordinates, whereas PRESET erases a dot at the specified coordinates.

GET and PUT together let you reproduce figures at several places on the screen without redrawing them. To begin, you set up an array with a DIM statement. After that, you read a rectangular area of the screen into the array with GET and send it back to the screen at a different location with PUT.

Determining how large an array you need is a rather complicated process. The following sequences will dimension arrays for medium resolution

```
50 ASIZE = 4+INT((WIDTH*2+7)/8)*HEIGHT
60 DIM SARRAY(ASIZE)
```

and for high resolution

```
50 ASIZE = 4+INT((WIDTH+7)/8)*HEIGHT
60 DIM SARRAY(ASIZE)
```

In both cases, WIDTH is the width of the screen area you want to reproduce, and HEIGHT is its height; these values are in points. For example, to reproduce a medium-resolution figure lying in an area 20 points wide and 50 points high, use this program:

```
30 WIDTH = 20
40 HEIGHT = 50
50 ASIZE = 4+INT((WIDTH*2+7)/8)*HEIGHT
60 DIM SARRAY(ASIZE)
```

Now, use GET to read the figure into the array. GET has the general form

```
GET (x1,y1)-(x2,y2),array
```

where (x1,y1) and (x2,y2) are the coordinates of the upper left-hand corner and lower right-hand corner of the screen area you want to read into the array.

For example, the following sequence draws two concentric circles around point (160,100) and then reads the figure for redrawing:

```
10 SCREEN 1
20 CIRCLE (160,100),40 ' Draw circle of radius 40
30 CIRCLE (160,100),30 ' Draw circle of radius 30
40 ASIZE = 4+INT((80*2+7)/8)*80 ' Find array size
50 DIM CONCIRC(ASIZE) ' Dimension array
60 GET (120,60)-(200,140),CONCIRC ' Read array data
```

Now that you have the figure information in an array (CONCIRC), you can display the circles elsewhere with a PUT statement. PUT has the general form

```
PUT (x1,y1),array
```

where (x1,y1) is the coordinate of the upper left-hand corner of the screen block you want to use.

Suppose that we want to redraw the circles around point (220,60). Since the outer circle has a radius of 40, we obtain the PUT coordinates by subtracting 40 from both 220 and 60. Thus, the correct PUT statement is

```
80 PUT (180,20),CONCIRC
```

5.3 COLOR STATEMENTS

Section 5.2 has discussed how to draw black and white pictures. Now we move on to color pictures. The PC's color options in the text mode are quite different from those in the graphics mode, so we will discuss each separately.

Text Mode COLOR

In the text mode, each character consists of two parts: a foreground and a background. The foreground is the character itself; the background is the box around it.

When you turn on the PC, it displays white characters on a black background. Furthermore, most television sets and monitors have a border area outside the area where they display characters. The PC initially makes the border black. However, you can change the colors of the foreground, background, and border with the BASIC statement COLOR.

COLOR Statement. COLOR has the general form

```
COLOR [foreground][,[background][,border]]
```

where *foreground, background,* and *border* are numbers that select the color for each area.

The PC can display 16 different colors. Table 5-7 lists them and shows you which numbers to use. You may use any color for the foreground and border, but you can use only the first eight colors (0 through 7) for the background. For those of you who are not artists, cyan is greenish blue and magenta is purplish red.

Once you select the colors with a COLOR statement, they stay in effect until you change them. For example,

```
10 COLOR 7,1,9
```

selects white characters on a blue background and a light-blue border.

You may change one color without affecting the other two. Here are some examples:

```
100 COLOR 0        ' Make foreground black
200 COLOR ,2       ' Make background green
300 COLOR ,,12     ' Make border light red
400 COLOR 14,,8    ' Make foreground yellow, border gray
```

Blinking Characters. You can make characters blink by adding 16 to the color number of the foreground. For example, *COLOR 18* (2 + 16) displays blinking green characters, whereas *COLOR 30* (14 + 16)

TABLE 5-7. TEXT MODE COLORS

0 Black	8 Gray
1 Blue	9 Light blue
2 Green	10 Light green
3 Cyan	11 Light cyan
4 Red	12 Light red
5 Magenta	13 Light magenta
6 Brown	14 Yellow
7 White	15 Bright white

displays blinking yellow characters. To turn off the blinking, use a new COLOR statement with a normal foreground color (0 to 15).

Graphics Mode COLOR

Remember, you can only display color on a medium-resolution screen. High resolution only allows black and white. In medium resolution, you may set the background to any of the 16 text mode colors (see Table 5-7), but you are limited to just six foreground colors. Clearly, this requires some explanation.

For medium-resolution graphics, the COLOR statement has the general form

```
COLOR [background][,palette]
```

where *background* may be any number in Table 5-7 (0 to 15) and *palette* must be either 0 or 1.

The *palette* value selects a group of four colors: the current background color and three foreground colors. If *palette* is 0, you can select a foreground of green, red, or brown, while 1 allows cyan, magenta, or white. Table 5-8 lists the palette colors.

For example, the statements

```
90 SCREEN 1
100 COLOR 10,1
```

set the background to light green and select palette 1.

Note that COLOR merely selects the palette; it does not set the color. You tell the PC which color to use in the statements that draw the figures: CIRCLE, DRAW, LINE, PAINT, and PSET. Table 5-9 summarizes their new general forms when color is involved.

Note that CIRCLE, LINE, PAINT, and PSET each have a *color* option. In each case, *color* may be 0, 1, 2, or 3 (the numbers in Table 5-

TABLE 5-8. MEDIUM-RESOLUTION COLOR PALETTES

Color	*Palette 0*	*Palette 1*
0	(Background)	(Background)
1	Green	Cyan (greenish blue)
2	Red	Magenta (purplish red)
3	Brown	White

TABLE 5-9. GRAPHICS MODE STATEMENTS WITH COLOR OPTIONS

Statement	*Action*	*Comments*
CIRCLE (xcenter,ycenter),radius[,color][,start,end]	Draws a circle or an arc.	Advanced BASIC only.
DRAW string	Draws an object specified by a string.	Advanced BASIC only.
LINE [(x1,y1)]-(x2,y2)[,color] or LINE (x1,y1)-(x2,y2)[,[color]],B[F]	Draws a line or a box.	B option selects a box; BF fills the box with the specified color.
PAINT (x,y),color,boundary	Fills an area with the specified color.	Advanced BASIC only.
PSET (x,y)[,color]	Displays a single point.	

8), where 0 gives the foreground the same color as the background. The *color* values 1, 2, and 3 select a green, red, or brown foreground if palette 0 is active or a cyan, magenta, or white foreground if palette 1 is active.

Since *color* is optional, you may omit it. The default is color 3: brown for palette 0 or white for palette 1.

For example, the sequence

```
90 SCREEN 1
100 COLOR 10,1
110 CIRCLE (160,100),10,2
```

gives the screen a light-green background and draws a magenta circle of radius 10 around point (160,100).

PAINT fills in circles, arcs, or line drawings with a selected palette color. Its general form is

```
PAINT (x,y),color,boundary
```

where *(x,y)* is a point within the figure, *color* is the color you want to paint the figure, and *boundary* is the color of the figure's edges. For example, to color the inside of the preceding circle white (color 3 of palette 1), you would add the statement

```
120 PAINT (160,100),3,2
```

Note that *boundary* has the same color value as the CIRCLE statement

(2). This tells the PC to paint until it encounters lines drawn in magenta. If you omitted the 2, the PC would paint the entire screen white!

Of the statements in Table 5-9, only DRAW has no color option. Instead, DRAW has a color command, Cn, that selects the figure color from the current palette. Since each palette has four colors, you may specify C0, C1, C2, or C3. Once you give a Cn command, the computer draws every line after that in the selected color.

5.4 COMBINING SOUND, GRAPHICS, AND COLOR

Now that you understand the statements that produce sound, graphics, and color, you should be able to write programs that include combinations of the three. As an example, Figure 5-6 shows a program that

```
100 CLS                        ' Clear the screen
110 KEY OFF                    ' Erase the bottom line
120 SCREEN 1                   ' Select medium resolution
130 COLOR 1                    ' Make background blue
200 '
210 ' Play "William Tell Overture" in the background
220 '
230 PLAY "MBT230MS"
240 PLAY "O2L8EEE4EEE4EEL4ABN38"
250 PLAY "L8EEE4EEE4N38N38L4BG#E"
300 '
310 ' Draw the target
320 '
330 COLOR ,0                   ' Select palette 0
340 CIRCLE (160,100),60,2      ' Red circle of radius 60
350 PAINT (160,100),2,2        ' Fill with red
360 COLOR ,1                   ' Select palette 1
370 CIRCLE (160,100),50,3      ' White circle of radius 50
380 PAINT (160,100),3,3        ' Fill with white
390 CIRCLE (160,100),40,0      ' Blue circle of radius 40
400 PAINT (160,100),0,0        ' Fill with blue
410 COLOR ,0                   ' Select palette 0
420 CIRCLE (160,100),30,2      ' Red circle of radius 30
430 PAINT (160,100),2,2        ' Fill with red
440 COLOR ,1                   ' Select palette 1
450 CIRCLE (160,100),20,3      ' White circle of radius 20
460 PAINT (160,100),3,3        ' Fill with white
470 CIRCLE (160,100),10,0      ' Blue circle of radius 10
480 PAINT (160,100),0,0        ' Fill with blue
500 '
510 ' Continue "William Tell Overture"
520 '
530 PLAY "D.E8DCDEF.P8"
540 PLAY "E2L8DO2BA4BA4"
```

Figure 5-6. A program that combines sound, graphics, and color makes the PC play the "William Tell Overture" through the speaker while drawing an archery target on the screen.

This particular target is constructed of red, white, and blue bands. We formed the bands by working inward; drawing one large red circle on the screen, then superimposing five smaller circles on top of it. For the blue bands, we used the background color.

Appendix A

FORMATTING AND COPYING DISKS

A.1 FORMATTING DISKS

Formatting a disk prepares it for use by the PC. To format a disk, proceed as follows:

1. Insert the DOS disk in drive A (the left-hand drive if you have two). Type

   ```
   format b:
   ```

   and press the Enter key.
2. You should see the following message on the screen:

   ```
   Insert new diskette for drive B:
   and strike any key when ready
   ```

   If you have two drives, put a blank disk in drive B (the right-hand drive); if you have only one drive, replace the DOS disk with a blank disk.
3. Press the space bar to tell DOS that you have inserted the new disk.

4. You should see the message

```
Formatting...
```

followed shortly by

```
Formatting...Format complete
Format another (Y/N)?
```

5. If you do not want to format another disk, press the N key.

A.2 COPYING DISKS

To copy a disk, follow one of the two procedures listed here.

Procedure 1: One Disk Drive

1. Insert the DOS disk and type

diskcopy

then press the Enter key.
2. The computer should display the message

```
Insert source diskette in drive A
Strike any key when ready
```

3. Replace the DOS disk with the disk you want copied and then press the space bar.
4. The next message should be

```
Insert target diskette in drive A
Strike any key when ready
```

5. Replace the original disk with a blank disk (the backup disk) and press the space bar.
6. Soon you should see the message

```
Insert source diskette in drive A
Strike any key when ready
```

7. Replace the backup disk with the original disk and press the space bar.
8. Repeat steps 4 through 7 until you see the message

```
Copy complete
Copy another? (Y/N)
```

9. Press the N key.

Procedure 2: Two Disk Drives

1. Insert the DOS disk in drive A (left-hand drive) and a blank disk in drive B (right-hand drive).
2. Type

   diskcopy a: b:

   then press the Enter key.
3. You should see the message

   Insert source diskette in drive A
   Insert target diskette in drive B
   Strike any key when ready
4. Replace the DOS disk with your original disk and press the space bar.
5. Now DOS copies the disk in drive A onto the disk in drive B and displays the messages

   Copying 1 side(s)
   Formatting while copying
6. When the computer has finished copying the disk, you will see the message

   Copy complete
   Copy another? (Y/N)
7. Press the N key.

Appendix B

BASIC COMMANDS, STATEMENTS, AND FUNCTIONS

This appendix reproduces the tables in Chapters 3 and 5, thus saving you the trouble of searching through the book every time you want to look up some detail. As usual, items in brackets are optional.

B.1 COMMANDS

TABLE B-1. BASIC COMMANDS

Command	*Action*
DELETE start[-end]	Deletes program lines.
EDIT line	Displays a line for editing.
FILES [filespec]	Displays the names of files on a disk. If *filespec* is specified, FILES displays all files that match the filename.
KILL "filename	Erases a program from a disk.
LIST [start][-end]	Lists on the screen the program currently in memory.
LLIST [start][-end]	Lists on the printer the program currently in memory.
LOAD "filename	Loads a program from disk into memory.
NAME "oldname AS "newname	Renames a disk file.

TABLE B-1. (continued)

Command	*Action*
NEW	Erases the program currently in memory.
RUN [line]	Executes the program currently in memory, optionally starting at a specified line.
RUN "filename	Executes a program stored on a disk.
SAVE "filename	Gives the current program a name and saves it on disk.
SYSTEM	Exits BASIC and returns to DOS.
TROFF	Turns trace off.
TRON	Turns trace on.

B.2 STATEMENTS

TABLE B-2. BASIC STATEMENTS

Statement	*Action*	*Comments*
	Print Statements	
LPRINT [expression(s)][;]	Prints expression(s) on printer.	Prints blank line if expressions are omitted.
PRINT [expression(s)][;]	Same as LPRINT, but displays expression(s) on screen. See also WRITE.	The symbol ? can be substituted for the word PRINT.
LPRINT USING x$;expression(s)[;]	Prints expression(s) on printer, using format defined by x$.	
PRINT USING x$;expression(s)[;]	Same as LPRINT USING but displays expression(s) on screen.	
WRITE [expression(s)]	Displays data on the screen.	Similar to PRINT, but WRITE puts comma between items and puts quotation marks around strings.
	Data Definition Statements	
DATA constant[,..]	Sets up constants that are accessed by READ statements.	Constants can be numeric or string.
[LET] variable=expression	Assigns the value of an expression to a variable.	

TABLE B-2. (continued)

Statement	Action	Comments
READ variable[,..]	Reads values from a DATA statement and assigns them to variables.	Variables may be numeric or string but must agree with DATA.
RESTORE [line]	Allows DATA statements to be reread.	
	Repetition Statement	
FOR variable = begin TO end [STEP n] . . . . NEXT [variable]	Executes the statements between FOR and NEXT a given number of times.	
	Unconditional Transfer Statement	
GOTO line	Jumps to a specified line.	
	Decision-Making Statements	
IF expression THEN clause [ELSE clause] or IF expression GOTO line [ELSE clause]	Makes a program flow decision based on the result returned by an expression.	If the expression is true, the THEN or GOTO clause is executed. Otherwise the next statement or the ELSE clause is executed.
ON expression GOTO line[,...]	Jumps to one of several lines, based on the result returned by an expression.	If value of the expression is 0 or greater than the number of lines in the list, computer continues to next statement.
	Subroutine Statements	
GOSUB line	Branches to a subroutine that starts at the specified line number.	A RETURN statement at the end of the subroutine returns computer to the statement that follows GOSUB.
ON expression GOSUB line[,...]	Same as ON...GOTO, but branches to a subroutine.	A RETURN statement at the end of the subroutine returns computer to the statement that follows ON...GOSUB.

TABLE B-2. (continued)

Statement	*Action*	*Comments*
	Keyboard Input Statement	
INPUT ["prompt string";]variable[,...]	Accepts variable values from the keyboard.	The optional prompt string display is followed with a question mark.
	Sound Statements	
SOUND freq, duration	Sounds a single tone of a specified frequency (in Hertz) and duration (in "clock ticks").	
PLAY string	Plays a series of notes according to a string of commands.	Advanced BASIC only. See Table 5-2 for string commands.
	Text Mode Graphics Statements	
CLS	Clears the screen and starts the cursor in the upper left-hand corner (row 1, column 1).	
COLOR [foreground][,[background][,border]]	Selects foreground, background, and border colors.	See Table 5-7 for colors.
LOCATE [row][,col]	Moves the cursor to the specified row and column.	
PRINT CHR$(n)	Displays character *n.*	
SCREEN 0[,[burst][,[apage][,vpage]]]	Sets the screen attributes for subsequent statements.	Only meaningful with the Color/Graphics Monitor Adapter.
	Graphics Mode Statements	
CIRCLE (xcenter,ycenter),radius[,color][,start,end]	Draws a circle or an arc.	Advanced BASIC only.
CLS	Clears the screen and starts cursor in the center.	Note the different starting place in graphics mode; center rather than upper left-hand corner.
COLOR [background][,palette]	Selects background color and palette.	See Table 5-7 for background colors and Table 5-8 for palette colors.
DRAW string	Draws an object specified by a string.	Advanced BASIC only.

TABLE B-2. (continued)

Statement	Action	Comments
GET (x1,y1)-(x2,y2),array	Reads graphics points into an array.	Opposite of PUT.
LINE [(x1,y1)]-(x2,y2)[,color] or LINE (x1,y1)-(x2,y2)[,[color]],B[F]	Draws a line or a box.	B option selects a box; BF fills the box with the specified color.
PAINT (x,y),color,boundary	Fills an area with the specified color.	Advanced BASIC only.
PRESET (x,y)	Erases a point.	
PSET (x,y)	Creates a reference point.	
PUT (x1,y1),array	Writes graphics points from an array onto an area of the screen.	Opposite of GET.
SCREEN 1 or SCREEN 2	Selects medium- (1) or high- (2) resolution graphics.	
	Data File Statements	
CLOSE [filenum]	Concludes I/O to a file.	CLOSE alone (without file number) closes all OPENed files.
INPUT#filenum,variable[,variable...]	Reads data items from a file and assigns them to program variables.	
OPEN [drivename:]filename FOR INPUT AS [#]filenum OPEN [drivename:]filename FOR OUTPUT AS [#]filenum OPEN [drivename:]filename FOR APPEND AS [#]filenum	Allows a file to be accessed.	
PRINT #filenum,expression[,expression...]	Writes data to a file.	See also PRINT# USING.
PRINT #filenum,USING x$;expression[,expression...]	Same as PRINT# but writes the data using format defined by x$.	For rules concerning x$, see PRINT USING under *Print Statements.*
WRITE #filenum,expression[,expression...]	Similar to PRINT#, but WRITE# inserts commas between the items and encloses string with quotation marks.	

TABLE B-2. (continued)

Statement	*Action*	*Comments*
	Screen Control Statements	
CLS	Clears the screen.	
LOCATE [row][,[col][,[cursor]]]	Moves the cursor to the specified row and column.	The final operand makes the cursor visible (1) or invisible (0).
	Program-Terminating Statements	
END	Makes computer stop executing a program and closes all disk files.	
STOP	Same as END, but STOP does not close files.	
	Date and Time Statements	
DATE$ = newdate$	Changes current date to newdate$.	The string newdate$ may take four forms: mm-dd-yy mm/dd/yy mm-dd-yyyy mm/dd/yyyy
TIME$ = newtime$	Changes current time to newtime$.	The string newtime$ may take three forms: hh hh:mm hh:mm:ss
	Define Statement	
DEF FNname[(arg[,...])]=definition	Defines a function that you write.	
	Random Disk File Statements	
FIELD filenum,width AS x$[,width AS y$...]	Reserves space for string variables in a buffer.	
GET filenum[,recordnum]	Reads a record from a disk file into a buffer.	Opposite of PUT.
LSET fieldvar$ = progvar$ RSET fieldvar$ = progvar$	Stores the value of progvar$ into a buffer, left-justified (LSET) or right-justified (RSET).	LSET and RSET are used to prepare for a PUT statement.
OPEN [drivename:]filename AS filenum [LEN=reclen]	Allows a random file to be accessed.	To close a random file, use the standard CLOSE statement.

TABLE B-2. (continued)

Statement	Action	Comments
PUT filenum[,recordnum]	Writes a record from a buffer to a disk file.	Opposite of GET.
	Key-Sensing Statements	
KEY(n) ON	Enables BASIC to check for function and cursor keys.	Must precede the first ON KEY statement. Advanced BASIC only.
KEY(n) OFF	Makes BASIC ignore key depressions.	Advanced BASIC only.
KEY(n) STOP	Same as KEY OFF, but BASIC remembers a key depression and will call subroutine as soon as KEY ON is executed.	Advanced BASIC only.
ON KEY(n) GOSUB line	Calls subroutine if key n is pressed.	Advanced BASIC only.
	Light Pen–Sensing Statements	
PEN ON	Enables BASIC to check for light pen operations.	Must precede the first PEN function or ON PEN statement.
PEN OFF	Makes BASIC ignore light pen operations.	
PEN STOP	Same as PEN OFF, but BASIC remembers light pen operations and will call subroutine as soon as PEN ON is executed.	Advanced BASIC only.
ON PEN GOSUB line	Calls subroutine if light pen is ON.	Advanced BASIC only.
	Joystick-Sensing Statements	
STRIG(button) ON	Enables BASIC to check for joystick buttons.	Must precede the first STRIG function or ON STRIG statement.
STRIG(button) OFF	Makes BASIC ignore joystick operations.	
STRIG(button) STOP	Same as STRIG OFF, but BASIC remembers joystick buttons and will call subroutine as soon as STRIG ON is executed.	Advanced BASIC only.
ON STRIG(button) GOSUB line	Calls subroutine if button is pressed.	Advanced BASIC only.

TABLE B-2. (continued)

Statement	Action	Comments
	Miscellaneous Statements	
MOTOR	Turns the cassette motor on if it is off or off if it is on.	
REM remark	Allows explanatory remarks to be inserted in a program.	To add a remark to the end of a line, precede remark with a single quotation mark (').

B.3 FUNCTIONS

TABLE B-3. BASIC FUNCTIONS

Function	Result	Comments
	Numerical Functions	
ABS(x)	Absolute value.	Magnitude of a number, ignoring its sign. Always positive or zero.
ATN(x)	Arctangent.	Angle is in radians.
CINT(x)	Whole number closest to x. See also FIX(x) and INT(x).	If *x* is not between −32,768 and 32,767, the computer generates an *Overflow* error.
COS(x)	Cosine.	Angle is in radians.
EXP(x)	Raises *e* to the *x* power.	*e* = 2.718282.
FIX(x)	Whole number part of *x*. See also CINT(x) and INT(x).	See CINT comment.
INT(x)	Largest whole number less than or equal to *x*.	
LOG(x)	Natural logarithm of *x*.	Natural logarithm is logarithm to the base *e*.
RND	Random number.	
SGN(x)	Sign of *x*.	SGN returns 1 if *x* is positive, 0 if *x* is zero, or −1 if *x* is negative.
SIN(x)	Sine.	Angle is in radians.
SQR(x)	Square root.	If *x* is negative, the computer generates an *Illegal function call* error.
TAN(x)	Tangent.	Angle is in radians.
	String Functions	
INSTR([n,]x$,y$)	Position of first occurrence of y$ in x$, starting at position *n*.	If *n* is greater than the length of x$, INSTR returns 0.

TABLE B-3. (continued)

Function	*Result*	*Comments*
LEFT$(x$,n)	Leftmost *n* characters of x$.	If *n* is greater than the length of x$, LEFT$ returns the entire string.
LEN(x$)	Number of characters in x$.	Unprintable characters and blanks are counted.
MID$(x$,n[,m])	The *m* characters that start at position *n*.	If *m* is omitted, MID$ returns all remaining characters in x$.
RIGHT$(x$,n)	Rightmost *n* characters of x$.	If *n* is greater than the length of x$, RIGHT$ returns the entire string.
SPACE$(n)	Inserts n spaces. See also SPC(n).	Value *n* can range from 0 255.
SPC(n)	Prints *n* spaces. See also SPACE$(n).	May only be used in a PRINT, LPRINT, or PRINT# statement.
STR$(x)	String representation of numerical value *x*.	Opposite of VAL(x$).
STRING$(n,x$)	String of length *n* composed entirely of the first character of x$.	
TAB(n)	Tabs to position *n*.	May only be used in a PRINT, LPRINT, or PRINT# statement.
VAL(x$)	Numerical value of x$.	Opposite of STR$(x).
	Keyboard Input Functions	
INKEY$	Reads a character from the keyboard.	If no key is available, INKEY$ returns the null (empty) string.
INPUT$(n)	Reads *n* characters from the keyboard.	Characters are not displayed.
	Date and Time Functions	
DATE$	The current date, in the form *mm-dd-yyyy*.	
TIME$	The current time, in the form hh:mm:ss.	

Appendix C

DOS COMMANDS

TABLE C-1. DOS COMMANDS

Command	Action	Comments
CHKDSK [d:]		
	Displays a disk and memory status report.	
COMP filespec [d:][filename[.ext]]		
	Compares two files.	See also DISKCOMP.
COPY old-filespec [new-filespec]		
	Copies files.	
DATE		
	Lets you change the current date.	See also TIME.
DIR [filespec]		
	Displays name, size, and date of file(s) on a disk.	If you omit the filespec, DIR summarizes the entire disk.
DISKCOMP [d:] [d:]		
	Compares two disks.	See also COMP.
DISKCOPY [source-drive] [target-drive]		
	Copies an entire disk.	Target disk need not be FORMATted.
ERASE filespec		
	Deletes a file.	

TABLE C-1. (continued)

Command	*Action*	*Comments*
FORMAT [d:][/S]	Prepares a disk to accept DOS files. The optional /S puts a copy of DOS on the disk.	*Deletes any files currently on the disk.*
RENAME old-filespec new-filename[.ext]	Changes the name of a file.	
SYS d:	Copies operating system files from the active drive to the specified drive.	Target disk must be one formatted with FORMAT d:/S.
TIME	Lets you change the current time value.	See also DATE.
TYPE filespec	Displays the contents of a file.	

Index

D

E

M

N

O

P